# THE SPIRIT IN THE LAND

**GISDAY WA AND DELGAM UUKW**

# THE SPIRIT IN THE LAND

Statements of the
Gitksan and Wet'suwet'en Hereditary Chiefs in
The Supreme Court of
British Columbia
1987–1990

**REFLECTIONS**
**Gabriola, B.C.**

**ISBN 0-9692570-4-X**

Copyright © 1989, 1992.
    **GITKSAN AND WET'SUWET'EN HEREDITARY CHIEFS**
    Second edition, second printing.

Cover logo: Ken Mowatt, House of Djogaslee
Inside logo: Vernon Stephens, House of Guuhadak/Yagosip

Published by **REFLECTIONS**, P.O. Box 178, Gabriola, B.C. V0R 1X0
        Telephone (604) 247-8685   Fax (604) 247-8116

**SMITHERS,
GITKSAN & WET'SUWET'EN
TERRITORIES**

**May 11, 1987**

. . . the land on which this
courthouse stands is
owned by the Wet'suwet'en
Chief, Gyolugyet . . . .

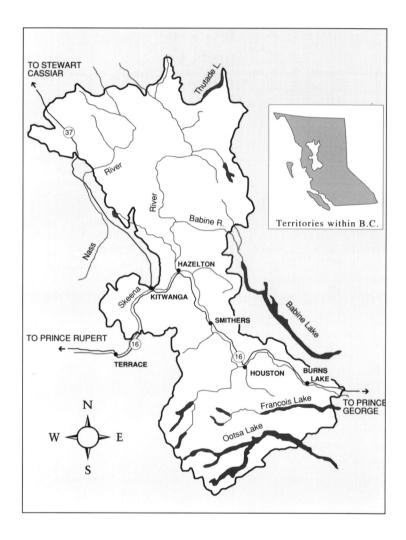

*Gitksan - Wet'suwet'en Territories*

# CONTENTS

# THE SPIRIT IN THE LAND

I n 1984, Gisday Wa and Delgam Uukw, on behalf of their
Houses and all other Gitksan and Wet'suwet'en Houses and
hereditary Chiefs, filed suit in the British Columbia Supreme
Court to force the province to recognize the existing Gitksan and
Wet'suwet'en title to their traditional territories. These territories
encompass about 22,000 square miles on and surrounding the
Skeena, Bulkley and Nechako river systems, and have been
occupied and protected by these nations for thousands of years.

The uniqueness of the Gitksan and Wet'suwet'en action
lies in the statement of claim. Not only are we seeking
recognition of title to the territories, but we are further seeking
recognition of the jurisdiction of our people over their own
lands. It is our belief that the Province of British Columbia has
no legitimate right to assert its jurisdiction over lands that have
not been surrendered and are thus, not under its control.

The process of settling a claim of this type is long and
complicated, even when all parties agree to negotiate in good
faith. The Province of British Columbia maintains a policy of
refusing to discuss these issues; this policy forced the litigation.
There was no perceptible movement or will to address the issue
on the province's part. Recent overtures on the part of the
Premier may indicate a willingness to move somewhat from this
entrenched stance, but we will have to wait and see.

The Gitksan and Wet'suwet'en people, in initiating this
action, have also found that they face the federal government as
a defendant as well. The federal Crown was named co-
defendant by the province, and notwithstanding its own policy of
negotiating settlements in such cases (and its fiduciary
obligations to native people) it did not protest too strongly. Both
the federal and provincial Crowns act in concert against the just
claim of our people.

Even with all of this, with spotty funding support equal
to less than one tenth of that of either government, the Gitksan
and Wet'suwet'en will triumph. We see indications that the
defendants are moving away from arguments designed to cast

doubt on the existence of aboriginal title, and are moving instead to attempting to lead evidence that would reduce the size of the area under claim. The people have won injunctions against logging companies such as Westar, to prohibit them from further destroying Gitksan and Wet'suwet'en land until the court case is over and the claim settled. Such injunctions recognize the authority and jurisdiction of the hereditary Chiefs. The people are active in protecting their land and resources and this determination is finally being recognized.

This first round in the Supreme Court of British Columbia will conclude with a judgement sometime in 1990. We will then move through the appeal courts, and we will be very lucky to be in possession of a final decision from the Supreme Court of Canada before 1996. This will be about 125 years after the date when the Gitksan and Wet'suwet'en people first made efforts to have other governments respect the sovereignty of their lands. It is a long process, but one we will win, for the colour of right is with us. In the courts, the defendants, the provincial and federal governments, also know this in their hearts.

THE HEREDITARY CHIEFS OF THE
GITKSAN AND WET'SUWET'EN PEOPLE

*Hanamuh, Fireweed Clan, Kitseguecla*
*From a painting by W. Langdon Kihn*

Photo credit: National Museums of Canada

# GISDAY WA SPEAKS

Smithers,
Gitksan and Wet'suwet'en Territories,
May 11, 1987

My name is Gisday Wa. I am a Wet'suwet'en Chief and a
plaintiff in this case. My House owns territory in the Morice
River and Owen Lake area. Each Wet'suwet'en plaintiff's House
owns similar territories. Together they own and govern the
Wet'suwet'en territory. As an example, the land on which this
courthouse stands is owned by the Wet'suwet'en Chief,
Gyolugyet, in Kyas Yax, also known as Chief Woos' House.

# DELGAM UUKW SPEAKS

Smithers,
Gitksan and Wet'suwet'en Territories,
May 11, 1987

My name is Delgam Uukw. I am a Gitksan Chief and a plaintiff in this case. My House owns territories in the Upper Kispiox Valley and the Upper Nass Valley. Each Gitksan plaintiff's House owns similar territories. Together, the Gitksan and Wet'suwet'en Chiefs own and govern the 22,000 square miles of Gitksan and Wet'suwet'en territory.

For us, the ownership of territory is a marriage of the Chief and the land. Each Chief has an ancestor who encountered and acknowledged the life of the land. From such encounters come power. The land, the plants, the animals and the people all have spirit - they all must be shown respect. That is the basis of our law.

The Chief is responsible for ensuring that all the people in his House respect the spirit in the land and in all living things. When a Chief directs his House properly and the laws are followed, then that original power can be recreated. That is the source of the Chief's authority. That authority is what gives the 54 plaintiff Chiefs the right to bring this action on behalf of their. House members - all Gitksan and Wet'suwet'en people. That authority is what makes the Chiefs the real experts in this case.

My power is carried in my House's histories, songs, dances and crests. It is recreated at the Feast when the histories are told, the songs and dances performed, and the crests displayed. With the wealth that comes from respectful use of the territory, the House feeds the name of the Chief in the Feast Hall. In this way, the law, the Chief, the territory, and the Feast become one. The unity of the Chief's authority and his House's ownership of its territory are witnessed and thus affirmed by the other Chiefs at the Feast.

By following the law, the power flows from the land to the people through the Chief; by using the wealth of the territory, the House feasts its Chief so he can properly fulfill the law. This cycle has been repeated on my land for thousands of years. The histories of my House are always being added to. My presence in this courtroom today will add to my House's power, as it adds to the power of the other Gitksan and Wet'suwet'en Chiefs who will appear here or who will witness the proceedings. All of our roles, including yours, will be remembered in the histories that will be told by my grandchildren. Through the witnessing of all the histories, century after century, we have exercised our jurisdiction.

The Europeans did not want to know our histories; they did not respect our laws or our ownership of our territories. This ignorance and this disrespect continues. The former Delgam Uukw, Albert Tait, advised the Chiefs not to come into this Court with their regalia and their crest-blankets. Here, he said, the Chiefs will not receive the proper respect from the government. If they are wearing their regalia then, the shame of the disrespect will be costly to erase.

Officials who are not accountable to this land, its laws or its owners have attempted to displace our laws with legislation and regulations. The politicians have consciously blocked each path within their system that we take to assert our title. The courts, until perhaps now, have similarly denied our existence. In your legal system, how will you deal with the idea that the Chiefs own the land? The attempts to quash our laws and extinguish our system have been unsuccessful. Gisday Wa has not been extinguished.

If the Canadian legal system has not recognized our ownership and jurisdiction but at the same time not extinguished it, what has been done with it? Judges and legislators have taken the reality of aboriginal title as we know it and tried to wrap it in something called "aboriginal rights". An aboriginal rights package can be put on the shelf to be forgotten or to be endlessly debated at constitutional conferences. We are not interested in asserting aboriginal rights - we are here to discuss territory and authority. When this case ends and the package has been unwrapped, it will have to be our ownership and our jurisdiction under our law that is on the table.

Our histories show that whenever new people came to this land, they had to follow its laws if they wished to stay. The Chiefs who were already here had the responsibility to teach the law to the newcomers. They then waited to see if the land was respected. If it was not, the newcomers had to pay compensation and leave. The Gitksan and Wet'suwet'en have waited and observed the Europeans for a hundred years. The Chiefs have suggested that the newcomers may want to stay on their farms and in their towns and villages, but beyond the farm fences the land belongs to the Chiefs. Once this has been recognized, the Court can get on with its main task which is to establish a process for the Chiefs' and the newcomers' interests to be settled.

The purpose of this case then, is to find a process to place Gitksan and Wet'suwet'en ownership and jurisdiction within the context of Canada. We do not seek a decision as to whether our system might continue or not. It will continue.

# THE HISTORY OF THE CLAIM

T he Gitksan and Wet'suwet'en, in asserting their rights of ownership and jurisdiction over their territory, are affirming the foundations upon which their civilizations are based and have been based for over 5000 years. In denying that these rights exist, the Province of British Columbia and the federal Government of Canada are denying the very existence of those civilizations. The foundations of Gitksan and Wet'suwet'en societies are firmly entrenched in their own laws. But in the face of provincial and federal disrespect for these laws and the injustice this has brought, the Gitksan and Wet'suwet'en have come to this Court to secure those foundations in Canadian law, law which the provincial and federal governments can be compelled to respect. Only then will the Gitksan and Wet'suwet'en be able to negotiate a just resolution of their relationship with Canada. This case is therefore a search for the legal pathways to justice.

This is not the first time the Gitksan and Wet'suwet'en Chiefs have sought recognition of their rights to ownership and authority over their territory. Indeed, their efforts span the last century.

In 1884, the Gitksan Chiefs of Gitwangak told the provincial government that the influx of miners to Lorne Creek within their territory, without their consent, was wrong and had to be stopped:

> From time immemorial the limits of the district in which our hunting grounds are have been well defined. This district extends from a rocky point called "Andemane", some two and a half or three miles above our village on the Skeena River to a creek called "She-quin-khaat", which empties into the Skeena about two miles below Lorne Creek. We claim the ground on both sides of the river, as well as the river

within these limits, and as all our hunting, fruit gathering and fishing operations are carried on in this district, we can truly say we are occupying it.

The district is not held unitedly by all the members of the Tribe but is portioned out among the several families, and no family has a right to trespass on another's grounds: so that if any one family is hindered from hunting on their own ground, there is nowhere else for them to go - they lose all the benefits they derived from their hunting, as they cannot follow the animals across the bounds into their neighbour's grounds. We would liken this district to an animal, and our village, which is situated in it, to its heart. Lorne Creek, which is almost at one end of it may be likened to one of the animal's feet. We feel that the white men by occupying this creek are, as it were, cutting off a foot. We know that an animal may live without one foot, or even without both feet; but we also know that every such loss renders him more helpless, and we have no wish to remain inactive until we are almost or quite helpless. We have carefully abstained from molesting the white men during the past summer. We felt that though we were being wronged and robbed, as we had not given you the time nor opportunity to help us, it would not be right for us to take the matter into our own hands. Now we bring the matter before you, and respectfully call upon you to prevent the inroads of any white men upon the land within the fore-named district. In making this claim, we would appeal to your sense of justice and right. We would remind you that it is the duty of the Government to uphold the just claims of all peaceable and law-abiding persons such as we have proved ourselves to be. We hold these lands by the best of all titles. We have received them as the gift of the God of Heaven to our forefathers, and we believe that we cannot be deprived of them by anything short of direct injustice. In conclusion, we would ask you, would it be right for our Chiefs to give licenses to members of the tribe to go to the district of Victoria to measure out, occupy, and build upon lands in that district now held by white men as grazing or pasture land? Would the white men now in possession permit it, even if we

*"...as all our hunting, fruit gathering and fishing operations are carried on in this district, we can truly say we are occupying it."*

Photo courtesy of Royal British Columbia Museum.

told them that as we were going to make a more profitable use of the land they had no right to interfere? Would the Government permit it? Would they not at once interfere and drive us out? If it would not be right for us so to act, how can it be right for the white man to act so to us?

This territory described in 1884 is the same territory as is claimed in this action today by the Gitksan Chiefs of Gitwangak.

In 1889, Chief Gyetm Galdoo from Gitanmaax framed his appeal to justice in this way:

There is land belonging to me and my tribe in the lower Delta, near the confluence of the Skeena and Haguil-get rivers. This land mentioned belongs to us, to times back as far as can be remembered. The land in question is part of our hunting, trapping, snaring and especially fishing grounds. A fish house is thereon and has been there for many years back. All this has been taken up by people not belonging there. Houses are hereon and more being built. Those people came there to erect a School House as a pretense, but turned the same into a trading establishment for the purpose of gain.

I strictly protest against all these proceedings and appeal to the law, to aid and protect me in this matter.

In 1908, Gitksan Chiefs travelled to Ottawa to present a petition to the federal government to stop the wrongful appropriation of their territory. In 1910, some of the Chiefs met Prime Minister Sir Wilfred Laurier at Prince Rupert. His response to them was clear:

The only way to settle this question [the Indian land question] that you have agitated for years is by a decision of the Judicial Committee, and I will take steps to help you.

In the face of the refusal by Premier Richard McBride of British Columbia to agree to any reference to the courts, which included the issue of aboriginal title, the federal and provincial governments established a Royal Commission to address the question of Indian reserves. In addressing the commission, the Chiefs insisted on talking about their territories and rejected the idea that their rights to ownership and authority could be contained or restricted to reserves.

Charles Wesley stated to the Royal Commission:

> I wish to tell you that this Reserve that you have just spoken about is something that we don't wish for...this country originally belonged to our ancestors - we were placed here originally by God, and it is only quite recently that the government has sent men out here to measure this land immediately around us, we were not notified of it when they did. Then the Provincial Government came in and sold the remaining land immediately around us...and what we most strenuously object to is that you insist upon us having this Reserve...I was one that signed the petition in 1908 which we sent down to Ottawa. We asked that the land which the Provincial Government has sold be returned or given back to us...this is where our inheritances come from and where they were handed down from generation to generation.

Efforts to have the courts address the issues of territory and authority were responded to by the Governments by amending the *Indian Act* in 1927, making it an offense, punishable by imprisonment, to raise money to press for land claims. That law was not repealed until 1951.

Recently the hereditary Gitksan and Wet'suwet'en Chiefs have endeavoured to resolve the conflict between Gitksan and Wet'suwet'en jurisdiction and the federal and provincial governments through negotiation. After a massive undercover operation by the Government of Canada against Gitksan and Wet'suwet'en fishermen in 1977, the Chiefs authorized an effort to negotiate a recognition of Gitksan and Wet'suwet'en management of the fishery on the Upper Skeena. In 1979 these negotiations came the closest to agreement when the Department of Fisheries and Oceans and the Gitksan and Wet'suwet'en Chiefs entered into an interim agreement, under which the river was open seven days a week except for conservation closures.

It was agreed that the Gitksan and Wet'suwet'en Chiefs would have to agree that the closure was necessary for conservation. Unfortunately, this breakthrough was short-lived.

In subsequent years although there were continued efforts to negotiate, the Government of Canada refused to recognize the Gitksan and Wet'suwet'en jurisdiction over the fishery and to negotiate as equal partners in its management. This continued even after the entrenchment of section 35 in the *Constitution Act of 1982.*

As an alternative, Gitksan and Wet'suwet'en people endeavoured between 1983 and 1986 to implement by-laws under the *Indian Act* which recognized the authority of the hereditary Chiefs. Finally, in April 1986 these by-laws were passed by the Minister of Indian and Northern Affairs. Once again, however, the apparent recognition of Gitksan and Wet'suwet'en authority was short-lived. In June 1986, the provincial government applied and obtained an interim injunction in this Court, prohibiting Indian people from exercising their rights to fish under a validly enacted by-law.

Some fifty years ago, the Gitksan and Wet'suwet'en registered trap lines in the belief that to do so would both protect their territories against encroachment and secure a measure of recognition of their authority from the province. Yet, throughout the territories of the Gitksan and Wet'suwet'en, they have seen increasing destruction by clear cut logging. In an effort to provide for some interim level of co-operation, the Gitksan and Wet'suwet'en Chiefs recently commenced negotiation with the province for a blanket trap line. This proposal would have allowed for joint management of the fur-bearing and animal resources, while recognizing that the Gitksan and Wet'suwet'en laws of succession would apply, and that the Gitksan and Wet'-suwet'en would determine trap line boundaries within the overall context of Gitksan and Wet'suwet'en territory. The Government of British Columbia withdrew from any negotiation, for the same reason as the federal government refused to negotiate on the fishery; for both governments, the Gitksan and Wet'suwet'en had no rights to the resources or to their management.

In 1982 the Constitution of Canada was patriated. Clauses protecting aboriginal rights were included. There have

*"...the provincial government...obtained an interim injunction...prohibiting Indian people from exercising their rights to fish..."*

Photo credit: Provincial Archives of British Columbia

been constitutional conferences at which representatives of the Gitksan and Wet'suwet'en Chiefs have been present in 1983, 1984, 1985, and 1987. The end result of these constitutional conferences has provided no recognition of the Gitksan and Wet'suwet'en authority and jurisdiction over their territory. Unfortunately, at the conclusion of the last conference in March 1987, it became clear that the Government of British Columbia would never agree to amendments to the constitution which defined ownership and jurisdiction of the Gitksan and Wet'suwet'en as part of their aboriginal rights.

The Gitksan and the Wet'suwet'en Chiefs have seen parts of their territory destroyed. This will only increase as large corporations build faster, more efficient, computer-operated sawmills which will increase the rate at which trees are turned into lumber and exported out of the Gitksan and Wet'suwet'en territory. The Gitksan and Wet'suwet'en hereditary Chiefs have watched their land being stripped bare. They have seen the destruction of fishing sites and spawning grounds and the extinction of salmon stocks. They have protested and resisted. Whenever possible they have enforced their own laws. They have continually insisted on their recognition as peoples with authority over the territory in which they have exercised stewardship for many thousands of years.

Johnny David, a Wet'suwet'en Chief, who has lived for approximately 100 years, was asked in his Commission evidence why the Chiefs have come to court. This is his answer:

> You can see throughout our territory all the stumps and the white people have pocketed millions and millions of dollars. All the money taken from our territory, we want that back and we want our territory back. Once we get back the money, we would like to go back to our old Indian laws to make life better for our people. The other hereditary chiefs as well as the other leaders are thinking about the same way and it is with their words and my words that I am giving you today. It is the generation that will follow me that will use the resources. I will not be able to use it. I am ready to go. (Johnny David, Commission Evidence, V. 7, April 22, 1986, p. 107)

Today the Gitksan and Wet'suwet'en enter the Canadian legal system to seek justice. This is an opportunity for the courts to find a just and lawful process to place Gitksan and Wet'suwet'en ownership and jurisdiction within the context of Canada.

If the courts provide no mechanism for a solution, then the people will have to guarantee the survival of their societies for themselves. As Delgam Uukw and Gisday Wa have said - they will continue to survive. The Gitksan and Wet'suwet'en and their laws are not going to go away.

But this Court can set the foundation for a resolution of the impasse which has characterized the history of the last 100 years. In coming to such a resolution, we urge you to initially set aside your task of determining appropriate remedies and concentrate on the evidence of the complexities and intricacies of the Gitksan and Wet'suwet'en societies, from which the nature of their aboriginal rights will emerge. It will be from this evidence that the legal pathway to a just resolution can be found.

# THE NATURE OF THE EVIDENCE

This Court, in hearing the evidence which will be presented in this case, will be faced with a series of legal and intellectual challenges and opportunities of a nature not normally found in matters that come before the bench. These are challenges and opportunities which we as counsel have had to face and with which we continue to grapple.

The Gitksan and Wet'suwet'en, in seeking recognition from this Court of their rights to ownership and jurisdiction over their territory, are seeking recognition of their societies as equals and contemporaries. The challenge here, both for the Court and for us as counsel, is to understand and overcome the tendency to view aboriginal societies as existing at an earlier stage of evolutionary development. The assumption underlying such a position offers persistent, powerful, and ultimately distorting conclusions as to the real nature of Indian society. The persistence of this assumption can be readily seen in the judgements of the Court of Appeal in the *Calder* case as recently as 1971. There, the Court stated in relation to the Nishga, neighbours of the Gitksan and Wet'suwet'en, "that they were undoubtedly at the time of settlement, a very primitive people with few of the institutions of civilized society and none at all of our notions of private property."

The sense of superiority implicit in such a statement is expressed in many different ways: as a function of social development that places the native people at the bottom of the ladder and western man at the top; or as a result of divine preference and appointment of Judeo-Christian religion as the ideal - with the corollary rejection of aboriginal shamanism and cosmology; or as a result of technological sophistication that entails obligations to improve the lot of other less advanced peoples.

Evidence will be presented as to the way these assumptions have been manifested on the frontiers of British Columbia within the territories of the Gitksan and Wet'suwet'en in the form of missionaries, federal Indian agents, and provincial government representatives.

A belief in white Euro-Canadian superiority has powerful implications not only in its devaluation of Indian societies as "primitive," but also in terms of their asserted rights to their territories and to their authority over their resources. If the white people of European ancestry are the representatives of the highest of human, moral, social, and technical achievements, then is it not right, and in everyone's interests, that whatever rights the Indians may have, be extinguished and vested in us? The links between moral, political, economic hegemony, and cultural dominance are not hard to see. We will be inviting this Court, through its rulings, to reject any legal theory of aboriginal rights which depends upon such evolutionist and supremist assumptions.

A second challenge for the Court, very much related to the first, involves the problem of communication between very different cultures. The problems here are not simply those inherent in the necessity to translate from Gitksan or Wet'suwet'en into English, as would be the case in a situation where the witnesses were Francophone. French and English cultures, although different, trace common and historical roots and share a world-view. The Gitksan and Wet'suwet'en world-view is of a qualitatively different order.

Anthropologists have long realized that a people's world-view is composed of two interrelated parts: first, the notion of how the world is structured, of how its parts have been fashioned into a cohesive whole; and second, a set of rules by which that structure is set into motion and of how that motion can be controlled or directed. There is a natural tendency, to which lawyers and judges are not exempt, to look at Indian societies using a model of the world that derives from Western concepts of the nature of the world and society. The dangers of this are that what Indian people say and do is either not understood or is distorted into shapes and concepts which deprive Indian societies of their essence. The challenge for this Court, in listening to the Indian evidence, is to understand the framework within which it is given and the nature of the world-view from which it emanates.

The Western world-view sees the essential and primary interactions as being those between human beings. To the Gitksan and Wet'suwet'en, human beings are part of an interacting continuum which includes animals and spirits. Animals and fish are viewed as members of societies which have intelligence and power, and can influence the course of events in terms of their interrelationship with human beings. In Western society causality is viewed as direct and linear. That is to say, that an event has the ability to cause or produce another event as time moves forward. To the Gitksan and Wet'suwet'en, time is not linear but cyclical. The events of the "past" are not simply history, but are something that directly effects the present and the future.

The nature of the continuum between humans, animals, and the spirit world, within cycles of existence, underpins much of the evidence you will hear. The Gitksan and Wet'suwet'en believe that both humans and animals, when they die, have the potential to be reincarnated. But only if the spirit is treated with the appropriate respect. If bones of animals and fish are not treated with that respect, thereby preventing their reincarnation, then they will not return to give themselves up to humans. In this way, a person's actions not only interact with those of the animals and the spirits, but also have repercussions for future generations, deprived of the food that will ensure their survival. Pivotal events in Gitksan and Wet'suwet'en history, such as the dispersal from Temlaxam over 3000 years ago, will be explained by reference to human beings failing to observe the prescribed respect for salmon and mountain goats and the spirits of these fish and animals.

It is important to reflect on how such a view of causality would be rendered conceptually from within a Western framework. Such a view would not be regarded as "scientific" and such attribution of events to the powers of animals or spirits would be characterized as "mythical". Both of these adjectives imply that what Indian people believe is not real or, at least, if it is real for them, it represents primitive mentality, pre-scientific thinking, which is to say, "magic". On either basis, Indian reality is denied or devalued. Their history is not real history but mythology. The binding rules which determine how Indian people should relate to animals are not real laws but primitive rites.

The interconnectedness between human beings and other life forms is only the beginning of the different ways in which the Gitksan and Wet'suwet'en see the world from those of us who are brought up in the Western tradition. The distinction we, as lawyers, make between constitutional, criminal, and commercial law are part of a vast array of distinctions such as those between law and morality, politics and economics, science and religion. Of particular importance to us are such fundamental distinctions between the secular and the sacred, the spiritual and the material, the natural and the supernatural. Many of the distinctions which we make in order to make sense out of the world are absent in the Indian world-view. It is not difficult to see, therefore, and indeed it is inevitable, that if we apply our distinctions without discrimination and caution to what Indian people say, we will make nonsense out of their evidence. The integration of what to us are discrete and separate parts of life, infuses Gitksan and Wet'suwet'en thinking, and permeates their most important institutions.

At the outset of this case it is important, therefore, to give the Court an overview of the evidence of Gitksan and Wet'suwet'en societies in order to illustrate this interconnection between the Indian world-view and the distinctive elements of these societies.

The Gitksan and Wet'suwet'en are two societies whose peoples, while speaking different languages, share many common elements in their social organization and institutions which they have, however, developed in their own ways so as to give meaning to their separate identities as Gitksan and as

Wet'suwet'en. Over the centuries, through intermarriage, adoption, trade, and the introduction of each other's ideas, they have forged their own distinctive form of confederation.

Both Gitksan and Wet'suwet'en witnesses, in identifying their place in their respective societies, will refer to their House and Clan. Houses and Clans are the two most important units of Gitksan and Wet'suwet'en society. A person is born into a particular House and Clan by virtue of laws of matrilineal descent. The four Gitksan Clans are Lax Gibuu (Wolf), Lax Xskiik (Eagle), Giskaast (Fireweed), and Laxseel/Lax Ganeda (Frog). There are five Wet'suwet'en Clans: the Gitdumden (Wolf), the Gilserhyu (Frog), the Laksilyu (Small Frog Clan), the Laksamshu (Fireweed), and the Tsayu (Beaver). Within each Clan there are a number of related Houses, which are identified in the *Statement of Claim*. These groups are called Houses because, in the past, their members would live under one roof. Over the course of history, some Houses, as a result of population increase and decline, have split off from or amalgamated with other Houses. In terms of the difference between House and Clan, a House is a matrilineage of people so closely related that the members usually know their relationship. In the case of Clan affiliation, there is the assumption that all the Clan members are related, although the precise nature of that relationship may or may not be known. As you will hear in the evidence, the relationship between House and Clan is complex and is differently expressed in the Gitksan and Wet'suwet'en systems.

You will hear how each Gitksan House is identified by its crests, images that encapsulate and provide a visual record of the major historical events experienced by the ancestors of this group. The Gitksan crests, *ayuks*, commemorate the group's origins, odysseys from ancient villages, moments when the people drew upon the assistance of spirit power, the defeat of neighbouring peoples who threatened their security, or the discovery of new ways to survive the natural disasters they periodically experienced. With the crest goes the *ada'ox*, the verbal record of the event. Key images within the ada'ox are evoked by songs, *limx'ooy*, that come out of the ancient past, literally from the breaths of the ancestors, to take the listener back in time by the very quality of their music and the emotions they convey.

The formal telling of the oral histories in the Feast, together with the display of crests and the performance of the songs, witnessed and confirmed by the Chiefs of other Houses, constitute not only the official history of the House, but also the evidence of its title to its territory and the legitimacy of its authority over it. The oral history, the crests, and the songs of a House are evidence, however, of something more than even its history, title, and authority. They represent also its spirit power, its *daxgyet*.

The witnessing and validation of the House's historical identity, territorial ownership, and spirit power is integral to the Feast. But also integral is the House's demonstration of its prosperity through a distribution of its wealth. A House's wealth is directly linked to its territory. In very early times, sometimes a cane was touched to the land, to signify the power of the Gitksan House group merging with that of the land, and the existence thereafter of a bond between the group and their territory. The cane used to forge the bond between the House and its territory foreshadowed the crest pole or totem pole. The pole which encodes the history of the House through its display of crests, also recreates, by reaching upwards, the link with the spirit forces that give the people their power. At the same time it is planted in the ground, where its roots spread out into the land, thereby linking man, spirit power, and the land so they form a living whole. Integral to this link and the maintenance of the partnership, is adherence to the fundamental principles of respect for the land and for its life forms.

You will hear evidence of pole-raising Feasts, including the Feast given by Guxsan within the past year. In the pole-raising Feast, the power which flows from the pole not only links the House to its territory and the life forms that feed them, but it also spreads out to strengthen the network of human relations forged by this and other Feasts. The power is shared

*The pole...is planted in the ground where its roots spread out into the land, thereby linking man, spirit power, and the land so they form a living whole.*

Photo courtesy of Royal British Columbia Museum

with all members of the House and feeds the other Houses and
Clans witnessing it.

In each each pole-raising Feast, the display of the crests,
the telling of the ada'ox, the singing of the songs, recreates the
historical events they represent.  This history is relived in the
Feast.  The identity and power it confers on the House group is
thus kept alive through its continuous recreation by each
generation.

Many of the Gitksan ada'ox refer to extensive migrations
of the Gitksan ancestors in the establishment of their territories.
By contrast, the Wet'suwet'en oral tradition does not detail the
immigration of the Wet'suwet'en into their territory.  As you will
hear, from the earliest time, they depict the Wet'suwet'en sharing
a salmon fishing village with the Gitksan and other groups at
Dizkle, on the Bulkley River, not far from the present site of
Hagwilget.  There, the Wet'suwet'en, like the Gitksan, lived in
large cedar-planked houses, presided over by a head Chief.  The
territory is described as belonging to a Wet'suwet'en Chief whose
people had the sole right to use the territory.  Thus, from their
most ancient history, the evidence will show that the
Wet'suwet'en identify their system as one in which territory is
held by a named hereditary Chief on behalf of House members.
The oral history, or *kungax,* depicts a series of battles until the
Chief decides to make peace by holding a Feast.  In this way, in
Wet'suwet'en history, the Feast was initiated as an international
mechanism for settling disputes and demonstrating ownership of
a contested territory.  Wet'suwet'en witnesses will explain to you
how, in a settlement of a dispute in a Feast, eagle down is
distributed to mark the binding nature of the resolution.  This
symbolizes that truly peaceful relations require respect being
shown not only between human beings, but also between human
beings and animals.

The evidence will show that the Wet'suwet'en kungax
operate on a number of different levels, the explication of which
will illustrate some of the subtle differences of the Wet'suwet'en
system with that of the Gitksan.  The word kungax is the
possessive form of the word *kun.*  Kun means "song".  It also

*...the power which flows from the pole...spreads out to strengthen the network of human relations....*

Photo credit: National Museums of Canada

means "spirit" or "spirit power". Kungax, depending on context, can mean a person's own spirit power, or his own song, or his personal crest. It can also mean a "trail of song". The Wet'suwet'en songs, which express the spirit trail of a Chief's name, and the enactment of personal crests, serve as a validation of succession to a Chief's name and its association with a particular territory. What the ada'ox are for the Gitksan, the kungax, the trails of song, are for the Wet'suwet'en. As the Wet'suwet'en follow the trails to their territories, so they seek to capture the songs that go with their titles to their territories. The songs link the land, the animals, the spirit world, and the people. The power of hereditary names and crests is continually renewed for the Wet'suwet'en by the highly personal and individual experience of being captured by song.

The distinctive Indian world-view has direct implications in this Court's understanding of the evidence relating to the nature of the Gitksan and Wet'suwet'en societies and their institutions, particularly those institutions through which the plaintiffs exercise their jurisdiction or authority. Societies marked by centralized government, such as Canada, possess discreet institutions and departments for conducting political life, economy, social welfare, education, dispute resolution, peace keeping, religion, and so on. Non-state societies, such as those of the Gitksan and Wet'suwet'en, do not have institutions which can be viewed as discretely political, economic, domestic, or spiritual; rather, their institutions simultaneously perform a multiplicity of functions.

This will be most vividly revealed in the evidence dealing with the most significant Gitksan and Wet'suwet'en institution - the Feast. While we will be referring to the Feast generically as the lynchpin or fulcrum of the Gitksan and Wet'suwet'en systems, it should be borne in mind that there are different kinds of Feasts to which you will be referred in the course of the evidence. These include: pole-raising, funeral, headstone, and shame Feasts. These and others collectively comprise the Feast system.

When today, as in the past, the hereditary Chiefs of the Gitksan and Wet'suwet'en Houses gather in the Feast Hall, the events that unfold are at one and the same time political, legal, economic, social, spiritual, ceremonial, and educational. The logistics of accumulating and borrowing to make ready for a Feast, and the process of paying debts in the course of the Feast, have many dimensions; they are economic in that the Feast is the nexus of the management of credit and debt; they are social in that the Feast gives impetus to the ongoing network of reciprocity, and renews social contracts and alliances between kinship groups. The Feast is a legal forum for the witnessing of the transmission of Chiefs' names, the public delineation of territorial and fishing sites, and the confirmation of those territories and sites with the names of the hereditary Chiefs. The public recognition of title and authority before an assembly of other Chiefs affirms in the minds of all, both the legitimacy of succession to the name and the transmission of property rights. The Feast can also operate as a dispute resolution process and orders peaceful relationships both nationally, that is within and between Houses, and internationally with other neighbouring peoples.

The Feast is charged with the power of the spirit world in the form of the crests used in the Feast and in songs and dances performed. Furthermore, the public and ceremonial emphasis upon giving, paying debts, recognizing and legitimizing the status and authority of the Chiefs and the ownership of territories, and maintaining the etiquette of reciprocity - all of these aspects of feasting are highly educational. By means of their practice, their repetition and re-combination through the course of the Feast, the essential values of the culture are both given expression and transmitted from generation to generation.

You will hear evidence how, through its many facets, the Feast weaves each generation into the fabric of Gitksan and Wet'suwet'en history and sustains them as they move forward into the complexities of their future. Despite the efforts of missionaries and Indian agents, aided by the legal prohibition of the Feast from 1884 to 1951, the Feast has remained a bastion of Gitksan and Wet'suwet'en societies. It has remained so because the system of ceremonial, reciprocal relations expressed in the Feast remains a model for everyday inter-personal transactions between kin, Houses, Clans, and villages, as well as between human beings and the non-human world with whom they share their territories. The transactions in the Feast Hall give meaning to what it is to be Gitksan and Wet'suwet'en.

This conjunction and combination of what, in state societies are seen as discreet, will also be manifested in the evidence of other institutions through which the Gitksan and Wet'suwet'en exercise authority over their territories. This case is brought in the name of the hereditary Chiefs. But these are not personal names. They are names which the Gitksan and Wet'suwet'en can trace back over the centuries and in themselves they represent the encapsulation of the peoples' history and its projection into the present and future. Indeed, some of the Gitksan and Wet'suwet'en hereditary Chiefs' names stand among the oldest continuously held titles that exist anywhere in the world.

You will hear evidence that on his or her succession to a high Chief's name, the person holding that name accedes to ownership of the House territory. As the proprietary representative of the House, the Chief has a range of responsibilities dealing with allocation and disposition of rights to use the territory amongst House members and non-House members. He also directs and safeguards the House's production components: the fruits of land, labor, knowledge, and skills, which are utilized in relation to the territory, so as to secure for its members and frequently for their relatives and in-laws, an appropriate standard of living. The Chief, as the proprietary representative, also has the responsibility for defending the integrity of the territory against the claims of other House groups or other nations. However, in addition to succeeding to the proprietary responsibility for the territory, the Chief also assumes a reciprocal stewardship of the land grounded in the people's sharing of the land with the animals, the fish, and other life forces.

As steward, the Chief is responsible for ensuring that the animals and the fish are accorded the respect which Gitksan and Wet'suwet'en law demands. Thus, by ensuring that salmon are not wasted, the Chief maintains his House's relationship with the salmon to ensure their annual return to provide for the needs of House members. In accordance with Gitksan and Wet'suwet'en world-view, if something goes wrong with the relationship, it is not considered an accident. In his or her role as representative of the House in the animal and spirit world, the Chief is responsible for determining the reason for the breach and for correcting it.

The roles of the Chief are not limited to those relating to the proprietorship or stewardship of the territory. Both within the Feast Hall and outside of it, the hereditary Chiefs mediate and resolve disputes between House members, between Houses, and with neighbouring Indian nations. Sometimes the exercise of this peace-keeping and conflict resolution role is highly visible in the Feast Hall; at other times his authority is exercised informally, operating through consensus and consultation. You will hear evidence of this process of consultation, involving elders and what the Gitksan will refer to as the "wings of the Chief" and the Wet'suwet'en as "the head push". These are the men and women who are the holders of other high names or titles within the House associated with crests, kungax, and songs.

The Gitksan and Wet'suwet'en Chiefs have another important responsibility within the overall Gitksan and Wet'suwet'en system when they are invited to the Feasts of other Houses and Clans - to perform the essential role of witnesses and validators to the claims to chiefly titles and territories made by other Houses. In order for Chiefs to perform their roles as witnesses to this distinctive form of public acknowledgement of land title, they are trained by their predecessors in the boundaries of their own House's territories, and the boundaries of the territories of their neighbours, and those with whom they are socially closest. They are taught to understand the power of the poles from the crests that proclaim the origins and the legitimacy of the House's right to possession of their lands.

There is yet more to the role of the Chief. The Chief inherits along with the Chief's name and the House territory, the crests infused with spirit power. Gitksan and Wet'suwet'en Chiefs exercise their authority and carry out their responsibilities with the aid of this spiritual power. In the course of the trial you will also hear evidence from the Gitksan witnesses as to *naxnox* performances which take place in the Feast Hall. Some of these dramatize the implications for a people whose members lack respect for the rights and territory of others and who lie, boast, or disdain their social responsibilities. If ignored, these dark qualities grow to become a destructive force that threatens the social order and welfare of the society. The performance is the ritual taming and controlling of this negative force, thereby creating order, peace and harmony. The Chief, as the embodiment of the House and the individual whose spiritual strength is most evolved, must use that strength to contain or mitigate these destructive qualities. The Chief, controlling one of these forces, takes on its name as one of his own. Each Chief, holding such a naxnox name, tames that anti-social force for his House and for the society as a whole. Naxnox performances of this kind can be considered an enactment of the process of civilization.

You will also hear about other forms of naxnox and the power of the *halayt*. You will also hear evidence that the authority of the Wet'suwet'en Chiefs derives not only from the assumption of the high Chiefs' names, but also from individual contact with the spirit realm which comes from dreams, visionary experiences, and what the Wet'suwet'en will refer to as *habo'stat*.

Clearly, the Gitksan and Wet'suwet'en hereditary chieftainship is a complex institution. In its perpetual succession, it shares the characteristics of what in the common law is classified as a corporation soul, the principal examples of which are the English monarchy and the office of the Archbishop of Canterbury. Indeed, the attributes and responsibilities of the hereditary Chief share some characteristics with both of these other institutions. The wisdom, judgement, political and moral leadership, spiritual strength, and stewardship expected of monarchs and archbishops are part of the attributes demanded of the Gitksan and Wet'suwet'en Chiefs.

In the course of this trial, you will hear repeated references by Gitksan and Wet'suwet'en witnesses to their law. Yet you will not hear evidence locating the power to legislate in any Gitksan legislature; you will not hear of any Wet'suwet'en Supreme Court House inhabited by a specialized judiciary charged with the duty of interpreting and applying the law; nor will you see any Gitksan policemen or Wet'suwet'en bailiffs who make their living enforcing Gitksan and Wet'suwet'en law. What the Court will hear about are principles and rules which entrench fundamental Gitksan and Wet'suwet'en values, establish a basis for social order, and provide for the peaceful resolution of conflict. In this regard, Gitksan and Wet'suwet'en law shares common features with the legal systems of all civilized societies. Although Gitksan and Wet'suwet'en do not divide up their laws and its administration in the manner of Canadian law, much of the evidence you will hear about their laws can be understood in terms familiar to lawyers trained in common and civil law. Thus, evidence will be presented which shows the existence of what we would call "property law"; rules which deal with the delineation and public recording of boundaries, the right to exclusive possession, the right to grant or withhold a subsidiary interest to use the land for a limited time and on conditions; rules which deal with rights of access to land by children and spouses; rules which deal with trespass and the right to protect the land from trespassers; rules which regulate the succession of property and which determine its alienability. Evidence will be presented of other laws which can be analogized to natural resources law, laws relating to the allocation of harvesting rights, and regulation of harvesting activities. You will be told about laws which are readily recognizable as Family Law and Succession, dealing with marriage, adoption, divorce, and the orderly disposition of interests in property and titles on death. But evidence will also be presented on laws which are not the subject of study in any Canadian or, indeed, Western law school, laws dealing with the appropriate conduct of human beings in relation to animals.  Environmental law does not begin to capture what it is when the Gitksan and Wet'suwet'en talk of the law of respect for the natural world.

Although Gitksan and Wet'suwet'en law represents a more integrated legal order than Canadian law, it recognizes what Madam Justice Wilson referred to in the *Motor Vehicle Reference* case, when dealing with section 7 of the *Canadian Charter of Rights*, as the "bedrock principles that underpin a system".  You will hear that the legal connection between a high Chief's name and territory is one such principle.  You will hear that succession to the name gives authority over the territory is another; that succession, the name, territory, and authority must be witnessed and validated by the other Houses is a third; that in exercising their authority, the Chief and all other House members must observe proper respect for the animals and fish that sustain them is a fourth.  Over the course of the trial these and other principles that underpin their distinctive system will be identified.  You will also hear in the evidence of the Chiefs the ways in which another fundamental principle - that Gitksan and Wet'suwet'en law be obeyed - has been repeatedly breached by federal and provincial governments.

The foregoing is an outline of some of the most significant aspects of Gitksan and Wet'suwet'en societies, their institutions and their systems of authority and ownership of territory.  Never before has a Canadian court been given the opportunity to hear Indian witnesses describe *within their own structure* the history and nature of their societies.  The evidence will show that the Gitksan and Wet'suwet'en are, and have always been, properly counted amongst the civilized nations of the world; that their ownership of their territory and their authority over it has always existed; and that they have shaped a distinctive form of confederation between Houses and Clans.  The challenge for this Court is to hear this evidence, in all its complexity, in all its elaboration, as the articulation of a way of looking at the world which pre-dates the Canadian constitution by many thousands of years.

We have so far talked about the challenges facing the Court in understanding the Indian world-view and the distinctive nature of Gitksan and Wet'suwet'en institutions and law. There is another crucial aspect of Gitksan and Wet'suwet'en society which bears directly on the nature of the evidence which will be presented to this Court. The Gitksan and Wet'suwet'en languages have not, until the last century, been written down. Their societies are in the oral tradition. The evidence in support of the Plaintiffs assertions of ownership and jurisdiction will include evidence of the Chiefs and elders in which they will relate the history of their Houses' territories and of their names. Their accounts go back to the most ancient remembered village and territory, including migrations or dispersal of the group to other villages and territories since then; they include an account of the major hostilities that took place when boundaries were being established or re-established. The significance of this evidence is that it will demonstrate the evolution of Gitksan and Wet'suwet'en society and the origins of the Clans, the Houses, the Feast, and the laws. It not only relates the essential elements of Gitksan and Wet'suwet'en ownership and jurisdiction to a time long before Europeans came into their territories, but it documents the depth of the Indian peoples' presence in and relationship to these territories. It explains the incredulity of the Gitksan and Wet'suwet'en Chiefs in the face of the assertion by the Province that the events of the last one hundred years have had the result of divesting them of their ownership and authority which they have exercised for more than five thousand years.

How should this Court view the evidence of Gitksan and Wet'suwet'en history stretching back over the millennia in the absence of the usual written historical record? Some assistance will be provided the Court in the form of archaeological and geological evidence which relates significant events and places referred to in the ada'ox and kungax to conventional "scientific" proof.

For example, the Gitksan ada'ox of Medeek describes the destruction of Temlaxam by a terrible force which ripped through the forest, bringing down trees in its wake and causing a rapid rise in the waters of a nearby lake. This destructive force is attributed in the ada'ox to a giant grizzly bear. The ada'ox describes this in graphic detail. Using the detail of the account in terms of the nature of the event and its physical location, "scientific" evidence will be presented relating this event to a landslide or debris flow that occurred in what is now known as the Chicago Creek drainage, accompanied by the damming of and rise in the waters of Seeley Lake. This event occurred, according to the scientific evidence, some three thousand five hundred years ago.

The Wet'suwet'en kungax of the House of Goohlaht describes its origins in the ancient village of Dizkle, where enemies had killed off all but one of the inhabitants and the lone survivor, a woman, unearthed, two and a half feet under the ground, an inert Chief Goohlaht, with a crown of grizzly bear claws on his head, the sign of being a shaman. The woman brings him back to life, marries him and together they build a new house at the Dizkle site, establishing a totem pole with a raven on top to warn them of any other impending attacks. This is the first Wet'suwet'en totem pole and the founding of the first Wet'suwet'en House. Archaeological evidence will be presented as to analysis of artifacts and contextual archaeological data from sites in the Moricetown and Hagwilget Canyons, which indicates continuous human occupation in the middle Skeena River drainage for at least six thousand years up to the present. Archaeological evidence of salmon processing activities, food storage facilities, large house structures, evidence of participation in wide-spread trade networks, and evidence of warfare, will be used to support the position that the cultural patterns of the Gitksan and Wet'suwet'en, as described in their oral histories, have been operating in their present territories for a long period of time.

Because we have no written contemporary account of the landslide at Stekyooden, or the founding of the House of Goohlaht, must the Court view the scientific, geological, and archaeological evidence as the only real evidence of the time depth of Indian occupation of the territory? Must the Plaintiffs own accounts of events which took place hundreds and thousands of years ago be deemed unscientific and mythical, mirages of reality, rather than the evidence of history?

For the Court, however, to deny the reality of Gitksan and Wet'suwet'en history except where it can be corroborated by expert evidence in the Western scientific tradition is to disregard the distinctive Gitksan and Wet'suwet'en system of validating historical facts.

In Gitksan and Wet'suwet'en society the Chiefs are responsible for their part of the society's history and for knowledge of their particular territory. However, Chiefs are reluctant to answer questions about histories or places that properly belong to someone else. It is as if to speak of another's territory were to constitute a trespass. As a total system of knowledge, therefore, Gitksan and Wet'suwet'en facts are shared out. The totality of the historical record exists in the minds of the Chiefs that feast together, those feasting together being those whose historical paths have crossed. In this way, the record of Gitksan or Wet'suwet'en history exists in its totality in the minds of those whose duty it is to remember it. Each Chief tells his history in the living context of the knowledge in others' minds. Thus, when a Chief describes the events that took place long ago, events that he or she could not possibly have witnessed, these can be told as established truths by virtue of having been tested and validated at a succession of narrations. These typically occur at the Feast where other Chiefs are responsible for ensuring that all that is told is told as it should be. Elders know that the important parts of their history, contained within the ada'ox or expressed through the kungax have been told, heard, and acknowledged many, many times. This accumulated validation lies behind the present day Chiefs insistence that a particular story is true and is not anything like mere hearsay.

In the course of his commissioned evidence, Fred Johnson, Chief Lelt, several times insisted that things he was saying were true because they had been witnessed and acknowledged. He used the Gitksan word *nidn't*, which Glen Williams, the translator at the time, rendered in English as "acknowledged," "confirmed," "witnessed". Translation of this term is difficult precisely because it is used to establish validity of a type that is deeply unfamiliar to Western ideas of truth.

For Chief Lelt, historical facts are facts by virtue of nidn't. They are confirmed by being acknowledged by a succession of witnesses who, thanks to their specialized training as high Chiefs, can be trusted to police distortions. We can thus begin to see the analogy between Gitksan and Wet'suwet'en nidn't-based fact and what, in other cultures or epistemology, is taken to be scientific fact. Western tradition distinguishes between what is experienced and what is hearsay; the Gitksan and Wet'suwet'en Chiefs make this distinction in a different but analogous form, by virtue of testimony and witnessing at the Feast. Western tradition distinguishes between an opinion and knowledge; an individual can have his views of any matter, but only properly qualified specialists or experts can venture to offer information that transcends individual opinion.

The test of the expert's truth in the Western scientific tradition has two facets: on the one hand, there is expertise by virtue of special training and discipline, while on the other hand, there is discovery and truth by virtue of testing hypotheses under controlled conditions. In the Gitksan and Wet'suwet'en system of knowledge, there are properly qualified specialists: hereditary Chiefs and elders, and they have responsibility for facts that are more than individual opinions. Also, a Chief has undergone specialized training and study, thanks to which he or she can be trusted to ensure that facts are stated and ordered in the proper manner. Finally, this stating and ordering amounts over long periods of time, often reaching far beyond the life-time of any single Chief, to a test of truth. By surviving in the Feast system, facts acquire a higher status, and come to constitute part of accepted knowledge - much as scientifically verified facts assume the status of knowledge in the Western tradition.

The difficulty we, in the Western tradition, have is in seeing the nature of facts in another, different kind of cultural arrangement. If one culture refuses to recognize another's facts in the other culture's terms, then the very possibility of dialogue

between the two is drastically undermined.  The challenge for
this Court in understanding the nature of Gitksan and
Wet'suwet'en validation of facts and in accepting Gitksan and
Wet'suwet'en history as real, is part of the Court's task in treating
Gitksan and Wet'suwet'en societies as equals.

The historical evidence which will be presented to this
Court is also intended to address some of the distorting cultural
biases with which we typically view Indian societies.  Even
though it may be acknowledged that Indian people have lived in
British Columbia for thousands of years before Europeans came,
that enormous span of time is viewed as a period in which little,
if anything, of historic consequence happened.  To the extent that
it is admitted that Indian peoples had their own cultures and their
distinctive ways of making a living, these are seen as static as
well as primitive.  In this way native peoples are commonly
viewed by Western societies as being without history.  As
recently as 1966, Hugh Trevor-Roper, the Regius professor of
Modern History at Oxford University, claimed that Africa had
no history prior to the era of European civilization:

> Perhaps, in the future, there will be some African history to
> teach, but at present there is none, or very little: there is only
> the history of the Europeans in Africa.  The rest is largely
> darkness...and darkness is not a subject for history...[which
> is] essentially a form of...purposive movement.

In the same superiorist vein, the history of British Columbia
begins for us when our ancestors arrived.  Part of this Western
historical perspective is that starting from the point of European
contact, Indian societies started to change.  The adoption of
European trade goods and the incorporation of new economic
opportunities, along with the incorporation of new religions, are
seen as a gradual abandonment of the real traditional Indian life.
This view of the nature of historical change has direct
implications for the legal issues in this case.  It has given rise, in
some of the judicial statements of aboriginal rights, to a
definition of those rights as frozen, as of the time of the assertion
of European sovereignty and European contact.  According to

this legal theory, the evidence must then be focussed on demonstrating the nature of the Indian society at that point, to determine the nature of their aboriginal rights. You will hear evidence from the Indian people themselves and from historians and anthropologists which will show that, at the legally relevant time according to this view of aboriginal rights, the Gitksan and Wet'suwet'en systems, and in particular, their concepts of ownership and authority, were in place. You will also hear legal argument that this test of frozen rights is misconceived.

There are other legal implications for this particular view of historical process which dates real "Indianness" to a point determined by European contact. To the extent that Indian life has changed, assertions of aboriginal title in the contemporary world are seen as historically and legally outmoded, because Indians are not now sufficiently aboriginal. There is then seen to flow from the inexorable course of history the abandoning of real traditional aboriginal life, and with that the withering of the *raison d'etre* for aboriginal rights. We suggest that this thesis underlies the real defence of the provincial Crown in this case.

We will be arguing that this Court should not endorse a frozen concept of aboriginal rights. We will be arguing that the entrenchment of aboriginal rights in the Charter is inconsistent with such a view. We will also be arguing that the aboriginal rights of the Gitksan and Wet'suwet'en are not to be defined exclusively by reference to some fixed notion of traditional Indian society. We will be presenting evidence that the division between traditional and non-traditional is false and misleading. It is misleading because it implies judgements about Indian life and culture that we would not apply to our own. These judgements also tend to place a form of cultural obligation on Indian people to live according to limiting and unchanging rules. The application of such a dichotomy denies to "traditional" cultures a right to be modern, to change, to evolve, to progress, and thus consigns these cultures to the past.

Evidence will be presented to this Court to support the position that the Gitksan and Wet'suwet'en systems are open and adaptive, and that many of the developments in their territories since white contact are not the symbols of their demise as Indian societies, but are a product of their vitality; many developments have been incorporated into an existing framework and structure of their society in ways which are a part of a chain of continuity with the past.

We will be presenting evidence describing the ecological and economic facets of the Gitksan and Wet'suwet'en relationship to their territories. That evidence will show how the major Gitksan and Wet'suwet'en villages occupy an ecosytem that is uniquely favourable to human habitation. Compared to the surrounding region, the mild, dry climate of the middle Skeena produces an abundance of food and plants as well as being best suited for the smoke-drying preservation of foods. Here are also found the most productive salmon fishing canyons of the Skeena system. This same ecosystem lies at the conjunction of three major North American climatic and biotic zones: the Pacific coast, the interior plateau, and the boreal forest. From their villages the Gitksan and Wet'suwet'en can efficiently travel to a wide diversity of rich valley and alpine environments that comprise their territories. This has enabled the Gitksan and Wet'suwet'en societies to sustain higher population concentrations than is normally found in other societies that depend upon hunting and fishing. These concentrations necessitated harvesting animals more intensely than is customary in such economies. This, coupled with the importance of trade, has meant that ecological monitoring, the orderly conduct of harvesting activities, and defined rights of ownership to territories and fishing sites, have always been important to the Gitksan and Wet'suwet'en systems.

The evidence will also show that trade has long been a significant part of Gitksan and Wet'suwet'en economies. By virtue of their location at the meeting of coast and interior environments and peoples, the Gitksan and Wet'suwet'en were actively engaged in trade long before the arrival of Europeans. From the earliest days some part of the food, clothing, along with much material culture, has been the subject of import and export between the Gitksan and Wet'suwet'en and their north-west coast neighbours. Trade routes and trails created a web of interconnection throughout the north-west coast. No one community existed in economic isolation, and the use or value of resources was not limited to its place of harvesting. Oolichan grease, an important part of both Gitksan and Wet'suwet'en diet, was transported from one river system to another and sold. Dried berries, dried seaweed, smoked oolichan, the meat of animals, dried salmon, all these figured in a trade in foodstuffs. Caribou and especially moose skins were also brought in, notably for distribution at the Feasts. Obsidian, used in the manufacture of tools, according to the archaeological evidence was traded into north-west British Columbia for some thousands of years. A trade in dentalia shells, also part of what the archaeologists refer to as the "tool kit," was also of considerable historical depth. This trade depended upon labour - the men and women who carried boxes, skins, and other goods from one community to another. At the same time, trading canoes moved up and down the Skeena. These were crewed, supplied and welcomed by various men and women of villages between the Queen Charlotte Islands and Gitanmaax.

It is within the context of an economy which was never isolationist, and which combined elements of domestic production and consumption with an elaborate complex of trading networks, that the more recent history of contact with Europeans must be assessed. Historical evidence will review the observations of the early traders, and in doing so, provide an evidentiary antidote to some well entrenched stereotypes regarding the nature of the relationship between the Hudson's Bay Company and Indian traders. The evidence will document the difficulties the early white traders experienced in their dealings with the Indians of the Upper Skeena because of the strength of pre-existing trading patterns. The Indians controlled the communication corridors and were jealous of their trading alliances. In order to participate in the regional trading economy, the Hudson's Bay Company had to fit into the ongoing system, contrary to the common assumption that it was the Indians who were brought within the encircling web of the Bay's system.

You will hear how Peter Ogden in his first journey to Hotset - the site of the ancient village of Kya Wiget and the present site of Moricetown - in 1821, identifies the Wet'suwet'en Chiefs by the names which appear on the *Statement of Claim* in this case and refers to them as "men of property". The observation of these early Hudson's Bay traders indicated that access to resources was regulated by a land tenure system in which tracts of land were managed by "the hereditary chiefs". The Chiefs, also controlled access to trails that traversed their Houses and territories. The historical evidence will demonstrate that while there was an intensification of competition with the advent of European trading enterprises, and some distortion in the Feast or Potlatch system, particularly amongst the Indians on the coast, in the interior amongst the Gitksan and Wet'suwet'en, increased trading opportunities were incorporated into an existing economic and social system.

The evidence will show that the participation of Gitksan and Wet'suwet'en men and women in new forms of economic opportunity in the late 19th and early 20th centuries, constitutes not discontinuous change, but evolution based upon existing patterns. Thus the evidence will show that with the increased volume of traffic on the Skeena, occasioned by the establishment of Hazelton as a major supply depot, Indian freighters formed the most significant part of the transportation network. When the Grand Trunk Pacific Railway line was built through the territory, Indian fishermen regularly sold fish to the construction crews. When white settlers began to farm the Bulkley, Kispiox, Skeena, and Kitwanga bottomlands, they quickly established arrangements for trading farm produce to the Gitksan and Wet'suwet'en for salmon. The development of logging and sawmill operations to provide poles and ties for white transportation and communication corridors, such as the railway and telegraph, are other significant examples of trade and exchange of human and natural resources of the Gitksan and Wet'suwet'en Houses and territories. The advent of opportunities for wage labour provided a new dimension in pre-existing exchange arrangements. Many people began to spend the summer months working in the fishing industry, either in the canneries or in the commercial fishery. This activity was again incorporated in the ongoing network of reciprocity, in that those who stayed at home caught and prepared salmon for those working on the coast, who, in return, reciprocated with store bought commodities and cash.

The evidence will show how these new forms of economic opportunities have been layered onto existing and dynamic economic systems. It will make clear that Gitksan and Wet'suwet'en economies were never based on subsistence alone. If we equate traditional Indian life with subsistence, the Gitksan and Wet'suwet'en have not been traditional since time immemorial. The absurdity of this kind of conclusion is some indication of how misleading seeking to confine aboriginal rights to some proto-typical definition of tradition can be. They blind us to the way in which Gitksan and Wet'suwet'en economies are open and mixed. The element of subsistence is part of a continual but changing economic balance.

By avoiding the mistaken and stereotypic implications of the idea of "traditional" subsistence economic life, the gain in understanding is extensive, for it means this Court can see Gitksan and Wet'suwet'en societies in the same kinds of terms as we usually discuss our own society. That is to say, by reference to institutions of ownership and jurisdiction of territories as socio-economic foundations. Societies without these foundations are properly understood as ethnic groups or sub-cultures. Societies with these foundations look to their boundaries and territories as the basis for well-being and identity in the present and future as well as the past.

So it is with the Gitksan and Wet'suwet'en. The rights which they assert in this case are ownership and jurisdiction over their territory and not to any particular economic form or way of making use of these territories. It is important not to misunderstand the implication of this assertion. Economic activities centering around the fishery remain to this day, as they

*...the participation of Gitksan and Wet'suwet'en men and women in new forms of economic opportunity...constitutes...evolution based upon existing patterns.*

Photo credit: Provincial Archives of British Columbia

have been for centuries, the economic well-spring of Gitksan
and Wet'suwet'en well-being.  This will be evidenced not only
outside of the Court by the enormous energy and activity which
will be generated this summer and fall by the Plaintiffs and their
Houses on the Skeena, Babine, Bulkley, Nass, and Nechako
Rivers, but also in the Court through the evidence you will hear
as to the efforts that have been made in the development of a
fishery management plan.  This plan, while building upon the
people's immense knowledge of, relationship to, and respect for
the salmon, integrates appropriate technology and "scientific"
information sources regarding fish stocks.  The use by the
Gitksan and Wet'suwet'en of computer technology in this regard
is not a demonstration of their abandonment of their cultural
inheritance, any more than the incorporation of new forms of
trade and labour represents a slide from a time of real and
pristine "Indianness" to one of contamination by alien economic
elements.  What the evidence will show is that there is a
continuity which relates the Gitksan and Wet'suwet'en to their
territories, and to their distinctive form of ownership of, and
responsible stewardship over, their resources.

The theme of continuity and change will also be
reflected in the evidence you will hear regarding the
incorporation of Christianity into Gitksan and Wet'suwet'en
spiritual systems.  This evidence will also demonstrate
something else - the determination of the Gitksan and
Wet'suwet'en to maintain their central institutions and laws in the
face of a concerted effort to stamp them out.

You will hear in the evidence that many Gitksan and
Wet'suwet'en are members of Christian churches.  You will hear
also these witnesses describe the continuing significance of their
spiritual beliefs centred on their relationships with animals and
the spirit world.  How can these beliefs exist side by side with
Christianity?  Is not the assumption of the mantle of Christianity
the assumption of the benefits of a progressive civilization and
the inevitable withering of "paganism"?  You will hear evidence
that over the past century and a half, the Gitksan and
Wet'suwet'en have integrated aspects of Christianity into their

systems and maintained both simultaneously. They are participants in Anglican, Catholic, Pentecostal, and Salvation Army churches; at the same time, songs, dreams, spirit power, and reincarnation continue to keep them in personal contact with the spiritual forces that have always animated their lives and which inform their practice of Christianity.

You will hear evidence that the introduction of missionary work amongst the Gitksan and Wet'suwet'en took place at a time when their peoples had been decimated by the introduction of white epidemics of measles and smallpox. In Gitksan and Wet'suwet'en cosmology there is no such thing as accidental death. If misfortune befalls a person and there is a death, someone must be responsible. Deaths by new diseases were no exception; the agent causing the death had to be located. The Chiefs and shamans - those endowed with special powers for dealing with sickness and death - were obliged to make some sense of, even if they could not minimize, the devastation that early contact caused. Part of that explanation had to be found in the fact that white newcomers seemed to be exempt from the effects of the epidemics. It is not surprising then, that the Gitksan and Wet'suwet'en saw missionaries as the white man's equivalent of their shamans. Nor were the missionaries slow to see the analogy and to use it to try and challenge the authority of the Gitksan and Wet'suwet'en spiritual authorities. Not only did the missionaries advance the theory that the Indians died because they failed to be Christians, they also insisted that Christianity offered eternal life. On the one hand, these new ideas seemed to explain the disaster; on the other hand, they seemed to offer an escape from its consequences.

The evidence will show that despite missionary activity and the diseases by which they were preceeded and aided, the Gitksan and Wet'suwet'en did not give up their own systems. In turning to, or accepting Christianity, the Chiefs did not abandon their own authority, rather they sought to supplement it or adapt some of its terms of reference. A major example of how the Wet'suwet'en incorporated Christianity within the context of their own system will be described in the evidence about their

)us prophet, Chief Kweese, who took the name of Bini.
ıto an ancient tradition of prophets amongst Indian
societies in different parts of North America. Indian shamans
responded to the influx of disease and the missionaries' message
about the death and resurrection of the Son of God by a
heightening of the shamanic role in which the shaman leaves his
body, travels to the sky realm, and comes back to reanimate his
body, bringing with him songs, dances, and prophetic messages
as to how the people must conduct themselves to prepare for the
changes that lie ahead. You will hear evidence of how Bini's
account of his ascent to Heaven and return to earth links the
spiritual journeys set out in an ancient Wet'suwet'en kungax with
New Testament prophecies.

You will hear how the Christian missionaries did not
share the ecumenical perspective of the Gitksan and the
Wet'suwet'en. Whereas the Gitksan and Wet'suwet'en were
prepared to accord Christianity and its practitioners a proper
measure of respect, the missionaries were not content with co-
existence. Their mission demanded an acceptance of the
superiority of the Christian ethos as part of the process of
civilizing the Indians. In this regard, the efforts of missionaries
and Indian agents, also bent on bringing Indians into the pale of
civilization, were well reflected in the legislative prohibition of
the Feast in 1884. You will hear evidence of the efforts within
the Gitksan and Wet'suwet'en territories to eradicate the Feast
from the fabric of Indian society. You will hear evidence of
apparent missionary success in persuading the Wet'suwet'en
Chiefs to burn their Feast regalia in honour of the Bishop in
1901. You will hear evidence of a petition of Kispiox Chiefs in
1914, apparently endorsing the prohibition of the Feast. But
these events, placed in their proper historical and cultural
context, will be shown not to be the acts of voluntary
abandonment, but Indian efforts to accommodate new beliefs in
terms of the form of the Feast without changing its essential
function. Despite the outlawing of the Feast, you will hear
evidence of the Feast given by Chief Nikateen in the 1930's to
protest the legislation. You will hear evidence of the Feasts held

in the 1940's. But the best evidence of the failure of missionaries, Indian agents, and the *Indian Act* to eradicate the Feast will be found in the evidence of the Gitksan and Wet'suwet'en Chiefs, that the Feast continues today to be their overarching institution.

The evidence relating to the history and nature of Gitksan and Wet'suwet'en societies will be led, not only in order to enable the Court to understand the Gitksan and Wet'suwet'en system of ownership and jurisdiction, but also to understand the response of the Indian peoples to the assertion of authority by colonial, provincial, and federal agents and governments. It is part of the Province of British Columbia's defence which they seek to support through historical evidence, that the Gitksan and Wet'suwet'en readily submitted to the arrival of the white man, his activities, laws and authority, and that in so doing, they have acquiesced in the incremental extinquishment of whatever rights they may have once possessed. This evidence relies on "primary" historical material, by which is meant the archival papers of the provincial governments, the diaries and correspondence of officials, missionaries and other private individuals. It is, in other words, the historical record and contemporary newspaper stories of those who live at the frontier and those who bring "civilization" to the frontier. Where it speaks of the Indian voice it does so through the distorting lens of superiorist ideology with its mixture of lack of understanding and disdain for Indian societies.

The evidence which the Plaintiffs will present, while dealing with many of the same events which are relied upon by the Province to show acquiescence and submission to Canadian authority, will explain these events in terms of the authentic Indian voice, and the Indian understanding of these events within their cultural framework. So explained, the evidence of "submission" and "acquiescence" will take on a totally different character. A graphic illustration of this, which will be referred to in the evidence, is the burning of the village of Kitseguecla in 1872, which may be regarded as the first significant conflict with whites. The fire was caused by a group of miners who had

neglected to extinguish their campfire. The resulting
conflagration destroyed 12 of the Gitksan Houses and most of
their contents, together with 12 crest poles.

As we have already stated, in the Gitksan world-view
there is no such thing as an accident. The persons responsible
must acknowledge their culpability and make suitable public
restitution. When this failed to materialize, the Kitseguecla
Chiefs blockaded the Skeena to all trading and supply boats.
The provincial government sent two gun boats to the mouth of
the Skeena and a meeting took place on board H.M.S. Scout,
between the Lieutenant-Governor and the Attorney General and
the Kitseguecla Chiefs, who attended wearing their ceremonial
regalia. The Lieutenant-Governor, Joseph Trutch, while
maintaining that the government could accept no responsibility
for the fire, stated that the government was prepared to make a
present as an act of grace to the people of Kitseguecla and that,
while the blockade of shipping would be overlooked on this
occasion, in future the rule of law must prevail. As reported by
the *Victoria Colonist*, the payment promised amounted to some
$600 and after its distribution to the Chiefs, the Indians "fired off
their muskets and sang songs expressive of their love for the
Whites". The ships guns were also fired at the conclusion of the
meeting and again, according to the *Colonist*, "the shot and
shells as they crashed through the trees or ricocheted through the
water seeming to impress the savages very forcibly with an idea
of the power of the Whites".

There is no *Kitseguecla Colonist* which we can consult
for the Indian account of these events (and the *Victoria Colonist*
did not have a regular Gitksan columnist on its staff) but the
Indian account has not gone unrecorded. In the archival material
of Barbeau-Beynon, a series of detailed interviews conducted by
an eminent white ethnographer and an eminent Tsimshian
ethnographer, we are provided with an important window into
these and other critical events relating to the early days of
Indian-white contact. Through a review of this archival
material, and an appreciation and understanding of Gitksan law,
the evidence will show that the meeting at Kitseguecla can be

seen in terms other than the affirmation of white law and order, coupled with a charitable benevolence towards the poor benighted natives. Viewed against this historical background and cultural perspective, the evidence will illustrate that the meeting on board H.M.S. Scout had certain elements of the traditional Feast. The Chiefs of the Kitseguecla Houses were there as well as the chiefs from Victoria; the Chiefs wore their regalia indicating their titles; there were formal speeches, food was distributed; there was a dramatic presentation of power accompanied by songs. In terms of, and in accordance with, Gitksan law, a settlement of a dispute was reached and witnessed, accompanied by demonstrations of power, payments were promised in recognition of wrongdoing and agreement reached that in future there would be harmony instead of discord.

The Gitksan response to the burning of Kitseguecla will provide this Court with an important insight into the nature of the Gitksan and Wet'suwet'en systems. They place great emphasis on respect and compensation. These two are closely connected. You show respect by sitting in your appropriate place in the Feast Hall as well as by abiding by rules for use of House resources. Failure to show respect, a breaking of the law, requires some form of compensatory payment. Compensation redresses wrongdoing symbolically, in the form of public admission of liability through a Feast, and then materially, often with payments of money, land, or in extreme cases in the past, with a life. The result is a negotiated settlement in which a wrong is put to right.

Throughout the history of white-Indian contact in north-west British Columbia, Indians have made many demands for respect and compensation. When whites break Gitksan or Wet'suwet'en laws, as the evidence will show they have done in cumulative manner over the last 100 years, Gitksan and Wet'suwet'en people have expected to be compensated. A failure of compensation demonstrates lack of respect for their system. Lack of respect for the system constitutes a further form of wrongdoing requiring additional redress. Indian demands for compensation cannot be interpreted as a demonstration that Indians, in return for money, are prepared to abandon their rights.  Payment, so far as it equals compensation, acknowledges and endorses the Indian system and is the very opposite of acquiescence in its demise.

The central role in Gitksan and Wet'suwet'en law of compensation and restitution has other implications in terms of some of the evidence this Court will hear.  When Gitksan and Wet'suwet'en elders relate what has happened in the past in terms of the abuse and disregard of their ownership and authority, they are not consigning their culture to history.  This Court should not see this as a lament for times and rights now lost, but rather a demonstration of the continuing life in the tissue of the system which causes elders and Chiefs to pay restitutional attention to the insult and injury of which much of recent history is composed.

The principal basis upon which the Province of British Columbia alleges that the Gitksan and Wet'suwet'en have given up whatever ownership and jurisdiction they may have had, is that they requested from the various Indian reserve commissions that additional land be set aside as Indian reserves.  The Defendant's thesis here is that by accepting reserves and seeking to add to them, the Indian people acknowledged the loss of their larger territories and accepted the reserves as a settlement of their asserted rights to those territories.  This thesis is the legal analogy to a commonly held view that the Indian reserve represents the symbol of Indian capitulation to European presence in North America.  To see the reserve as such a symbol is to imply a particular historical process: Indians once had their territories, nowadays they have their reserves.  This alleged continuum of ever contracting land contains a stereotype which is closely allied to the evolutionism which we have already brought to the attention of this Court; the roaming hunter, with the life of limitless freedom that comes with dependence only on subsistence resources is progressively confined.  There is a perceived inexorable logic that Indians who once had territories in their "traditional" life now have the remnants of those territories, their reserves, matching the remnants of their "traditional" culture. There are further corollaries to this view. The reserves are those places which we have given them, so we acknowledge them to be their lands. On this view, the rest of the land is not theirs, but ours.

Gitksan and Wet'suwet'en reserve lands amount to some 45 square miles. The thesis embodied in paragraph 34 of the Province's *Statement of Defence* is that the Gitksan and Wet'suwet'en villages that make up most of the 45 square miles, represent the fitting conclusion of this historical process. The Plaintiffs will be presenting to this Court extensive evidence relating to the establishment of Indian reserves and the Gitksan's and Wet'suwet'en's responses to this process. That evidence will show that Gitksan and Wet'suwet'en Chiefs have always rejected the reserve system and that this rejection is a thread that runs through, and in many ways ties together, many of the key events of this century. Gitksan and Wet'suwet'en life never could, and never did, allow itself to be confined to a small set of reserve lands.

You will hear much evidence relating to the establishment of the *McKenna-McBride Agreement* and the ensuing *McKenna-McBride Commission* (also known as the *Royal Commission on Indian Affairs for the Province of British Columbia*) which held hearings throughout British Columbia between 1912-15. The circumstances leading up to the Agreement are of great significance to this case, linking together as they do a period of accelerating Indian protest and assertion of their aboriginal rights to their territories, including petitions to the English Crown and efforts to obtain a judicial ruling from the Privy Council. They also prove an important window into provincial and federal responses to these initiatives which, in the form of the *McKenna-McBride Agreement,* resulted in an accord to deal only with the resolution of outstanding federal-provincial issues relating to Indian reserve lands and specifically excluded any determination of the issue of aboriginal rights. That issue was to be set aside for future consideration. As you will hear later, this was not the first nor the last occasion in which, in the spirit of co-operative federalism, a principled resolution of Indian rights was deferred.

In the extensive hearings which the *McKenna-McBride Royal Commission* conducted across the province, Indian attempts to raise the issue of aboriginal title were met with the response by the Commissioners that this was beyond the Commission's terms of reference. Of great relevance to the position taken by the Province in its Defence, is the assurance Indian witnesses were given that participation in the work of the Commission would not prejudice their claims based on aboriginal title. Thus you will hear evidence of the following exchange between the Chairman of the *Royal Commission* and William Holland, Chief Haalus, at the meeting with the Kuldoe Band. William Holland is the father of Mary Mackenzie, Chief Gyolugyet, the first witness we will be calling.

> William Holland:...The Chief wants me to speak for him...we just want one thing and that is to get back our land again - the land was here before we were here and we want to get it back - all the land along the Skeena River.

> The Chairman:...Some of the Indians, and those who are supporting your claim, thought at one time that if you applied to us for certain lands and we gave them to you that you were, to some extent, giving up some of your privileges; that if you accepted those lands you would not have the further right to take this matter up in the Courts, but a further Order-in-Council was passed expressly stating that this would not affect you in the least.

Paragraph 34 of the Province's *Statement of Defence* would seek to make a liar out of the Chairman of this *Royal Commission*.

The evidence of Gitksan and Wet'suwet'en Chiefs at the *Royal Commission* hearings is significant in understanding Indian attitudes to reserves. You have already been referred to the statement that Charles Wesley made to the Commission:

I wish to tell you that this Reserve that you have just spoken about is something that we don't wish for....This country originally belonged to our ancestors - we were placed here originally by God, and it is only quite recently that the government has sent men out here to measure this land immediately around us, we were not notified of it when they did. Then the provincial government came in and sold the remaining land immediately around us...and what we most strenuously object to is that you insist upon us having this Reserve....I was one that signed the petition in 1908 which we sent down to Ottawa. We asked that the land which the provincial government had sold be returned or given back to us....This is where our inheritances come from and where they were handed down from generation to generation.

You will also hear evidence of the exchange between the Commission and one of the Hagwilget Chiefs:

If you want to help us there is only three things we want and that's the first thing just people dead. It's just the same thing as tying them up and letting them die.

The Commissioner's response to this was:

You mean that to restrict or confine the Indians to their Reserves, you mean that is killing you?

The Chief's answer was simple and affirmative.

The evidence you will hear will leave you in no doubt that the Gitksan Chiefs' statements to the *Royal Commission* stand as a testament to the affirmation of their rights to their territory and not their voluntary participation in their own demise.

Evidence will be presented to this Court as to the role that the Gitksan and Wet'suwet'en reserves play in Indian life in order for the Court to understand that they are not the capital of a residual Indian culture. Many of the reserves are ancient village sites, where Indian people have chosen to spend at least part of each year over a period of centuries, and in some cases, millennia. They include Kitwanga, Kitseguecla, Kispiox, Kisgagas, Kuldoe, Gitanmaax, Hagwilget, and Moricetown. Other reserves such as Glen Vowell are places which missionaries thought were a good place for Indians to relocate. Indian agents and missionaries encouraged Indians to move to, or remain living all year round on reserves through a set of incentives, in the expectation that ultimately and inevitably Indians would become like us.

But the evidence you hear will show that reserves were never seen nor accepted by the Gitksan or Wet'suwet'en as centres of assimilation. Conceived by the early Indian agents as a legal and administrative fence to confine, control, and monitor Indians, the reserve has never succeeded in confining the Gitksan and Wet'suwet'en culture and economy within its limits. The evidence of the activities of each historical period will show this failure. The ever-developing round of Gitksan and Wet'suwet'en economic life, most notably in the growth of the mixed economy, for example, the inclusion of small scale logging and sawmill operations, will indicate that Gitksan and Wet'suwet'en life was not confined to the reserve in the 1940's and 50's. The importance of trapping for so many Gitksan and Wet'suwet'en families shows that there was no such confinement in the 1930's. The way in which the many threads of Gitksan and Wet'suwet'en life led people and produce along trails, that criss-cross through the territories, shows the active life of the cultures beyond reserves in the 1920's. The transcripts of the *McKenna-McBride Commission* show that Indian people regarded the intention to confine them to reserves as an affront and an unacceptable offence against Gitksan and Wet'suwet'en life and culture. The land claims process, and, ultimately, this court case itself, reveals the extent to which the Gitksan and Wet'suwet'en have refused to accept the ideas implicit in the reserve system.

The boundaries of the Gitksan and Wet'suwet'en territories are not to be found by reference to the surveyed limits of their reserves. Those boundaries, for many generations, have been and are still being proclaimed and validated in the Feast Hall. For the benefit of this Court they have been set out in maps. As you will hear, in preparing these maps, the Chiefs went out into their territories and from the mountain tops pointed out to the researchers and map makers the metes and bounds of those territories. From up there the reserves assumed their proper significance. The Plaintiffs in the course of their evidence in this case will, in effect, "walk" the Court around their territories as part of the process to obtain this Court's acknowledgement of what to them has never been in dispute: that these territories are Gitksan and Wet'suwet'en.

In the same way it is essential that this Court has a clear understanding of the place of reserves in Indian life in order to address the legal issues raised in the *Statement of Defence,* so also it must come to understand the issue of trap lines and trap line registration. These terms are charged with legal significance. Trap lines are registered under provincial legislation and the system is administered by provincial officials. Does it not follow, therefore, as argued by the Defendants, that a Gitksan or Wet'suwet'en Chief who has registered the trap line has, as it were, "attorned" to provincial authority and voluntarily surrendered whatever aboriginal rights he or she may have had in return for a provincial grant? The evidence the Plaintiffs will be presenting will show that trap line registration, far from an "attornment" to provincial jurisdiction, was an attempt by the Gitksan and Wet'suwet'en to seek a measure of recognition from the provincial government of their rights to their Houses' territories. The evidence will show that trap line registration was introduced by the provincial government in the 1920's, as part of a practical solution to wildlife resource problems emerging out of the changing frontier. The registration system, together with the game legislation, was the first component in an evolving attempt to manage the wildlife resources in concert with new agricultural and other economic activities. The evidence will show that federal Indian agents actively encouraged Indians to register trap lines by informing them that unless they did, their territories would be taken up by whites, with the resultant loss of their hunting and trapping economy. Many Indians were also given to understand that registration would make no difference to their existing rights. The evidence will show that registration of a trap line was understood by the Gitksan and Wet'suwet'en to reinforce and underpin their aboriginal rights. Informed by an understanding of the nature of the Gitksan and Wet'suwet'en system, the evidence will explain why this would be so. Provincial officials did not come to the Feast Hall, the proper and legal forum for dealing with rights to territories; therefore, the Chiefs, concerned about their territories, must find whatever means they can to establish publicly and officially that they own their lands. Trap line registration, therefore, was seen within the legal logic of their own system as a form of validation of their rights and authority.

The confusion between white and Indian views of trap line registration will be revealed in the course of the evidence by the interchangeability of the terms, "trap line" and "hunting territories". Indians registered at least a part of their land, without giving up their claim to own and manage the whole of it. The term "trap line" is generally used to refer to the territory as a whole. Registration maps, other documents, and the peoples' own accounts, will show a high degree of correspondence between areas registered and hereditary House territories. In addition, the evidence will show that many Chiefs registered a "company" or group (in effect, a House) rather than an individual name, facts which support the conclusion that registration was undertaken within the existing Gitksan and Wet'suwet'en system.

Trap line registration, properly understood in its historical and cultural context, can be seen as an attempt by the Gitksan and Wet'suwet'en to accommodate and incorporate certain aspects of Canadian law as a measure of protection for their ownership and authority. You will hear how this has resulted in strains upon their existing system. The most significant of these has been the result of differences in provincial and Indian laws of succession. As we have explained, under Gitksan and Wet'suwet'en law, ownership and authority of a House's territory descends with the hereditary Chief's name through a matrilineal system. Under provincial law, trap lines are inherited patrilineally from father to son. You will hear evidence of how the Gitksan and Wet'suwet'en have attempted to deal with this conflict of laws. They have not turned to Professor Cheshire to seek the answer in his text on private international law, rather they have drawn upon the dynamic quality of their own system to seek to resolve these problems.

The efforts at resolution themselves require an understanding of that system. Although we have referred to the principle of matrilineal succession as an essential feature of Gitksan and Wet'suwet'en law, this does not mean that "the father's side", that is, the father's House and Clan, are legally or socially irrelevant. Indeed you will hear much evidence how the father's House has important legal and social responsibilities towards the father's children, both within and outside the Feast Hall. While the children cannot inherit the House's territory from their father, they are accorded rights of access to that territory during his lifetime. That access can be renewed after his death. It is within the context of this existing reciprocity between the father's side and the mother's side that the problems of trap line registration have been addressed.

You will hear evidence of individuals who, as a result of succession to a trap line under the provincial system, use territories which rightfully belong to another House and do so as caretakers, acknowledging the legitimacy of the title of the rightful owners. The Wet'suwet'en term for this, *negedel des,* means "we are here frying something". Amongst the Gitksan this relationship is called *am nig wootxw*, or "the privilege granted to the father's children".

The problems inherent in trap line registration have, in many cases, been mitigated by the pattern of intermarriage between two Houses, as a result of which, over time these interacting Houses will be "feeding" each other's children from their own respective territories in alternate generations. All of this is not to say that all of the conflict between provincial and

Indian law has been resolved.  Indeed, the very fact of conflict and ongoing attempts to resolve these within the context of the Feast Hall, is the best evidence of the continuing vitality of the Indian system.

The thrust of what we have said about the evidence we will be leading on the issues of reserves and trap lines is that the Gitksan and Wet'suwet'en have not voluntarily surrendered nor have they acquiesced in the abridgement of those rights.  But voluntary surrender and acquiescence are only part of the defence of the Province of British Columbia.  In paragraph 36 of the Defence, the Province pleads that whatever aboriginal rights the Plaintiffs may have had, those rights were reduced, diminished, or extinguished by the Colony and Province of British Columbia through: the making or enactment of laws of general application, by administrative actions pursuant to such laws, and by the actions of third parties in the exercise of rights and privileges conferred thereby.

As we understand this defence, it is that the rights have been granted by the colonial and provincial governments under various land and pre-emption proclamations, ordinances, and acts, as a result of which third parties have entered into possession of lands claimed by the Plaintiffs.  This process, as a matter of law, has extinguished the Plaintiffs' asserted rights.  Underlying this defence is a certain view of realpolitik which can be set out in this way.  The Province of British Columbia has made grants to Indian land on the basis that Indian people had no rights.  The parties to whom the grants were made have taken up these lands and treated them as their own.  If Indian people in fact did have rights, it is now too late to turn back the clock and, therefore, as a matter of law those rights must be held to have been extinguished.  Under this thesis, the more blatant in fact the disregard for Indian rights, the more self-evident in law it is that those rights be disregarded.  In this way injustice, like virtue, can be its own reward.

We will have much to say about the legal bankruptcy of the Province's position in our legal argument.  The Province will be presenting evidence in the form of detailed maps describing

the extent of their alienations within the Gitksan and
Wet'suwet'en territory. The Plaintiffs also will be presenting
evidence on the process of alienation in order to re-create in this
courtroom the dark reality of what lies behind the Province's
colour-coded maps.

The Court's attention will be directed particularly to
evidence of what took place at the beginning of this century in
the Bulkley Valley on the territories of the Wet'suwet'en Chiefs.
The evidence will show how, between the years 1901 and 1905,
a considerable amount of prime land in the Upper Skeena and
Bulkley Valley regions was conveyed by the Province to private
parties through the vehicle of the South African war scrip.
Under this scheme, a volunteer from British Columbia who
served in the Boer War was eligible to receive scrip which
entitled him to take up 160 acres of "unoccupied, unclaimed and
unreserved Crown land" anywhere in the province. The scrip
could also be sold. Because of the way the legislation was
drafted, many veterans could not, or chose not, to use the scrip to
take up land. You will read the letter of one such veteran, Mr.
Dobie, who, describing the legislation, stated: "If the
government had studied to devise a scheme by which a large
area of land would be turned over to the hungry 'land sharks' no
more effective scheme could have been adopted".

In fact, much of the scrip was rapidly acquired by a
small number of large-scale land speculators. Mr. Dobie's scrip
was purchased by one of the larger dealers in South African
scrip and was used to acquire a quarter section of land in the
Bulkley Valley, land which became the town site of Telkwa.
Scrip was frequently resold to smaller investors, some of whom
held either the scrip or the land, waiting for it to appreciate in
value. In this way, title to considerable areas of land were held
by absentee owners for years before there was any attempt at
actual entry or settlement.

Through the medium of South African war scrip, a paper
transfer of title to many quarter sections of land in the Bulkley
Valley was effected while the Wet'suwet'en Houses continued to
use these territories, unaware of any purported changes or

transfers in ownership.  In many cases, the Wet'suwet'en did not learn until years afterward that the Province had "alienated" the land by issuing Crown grants.

The use of South African war scrip to take up land in the Bulkley Valley should not have resulted in the dispossession of Indian families.  Under the legislation only unoccupied, unclaimed and unreserved land was available.  When lands were surveyed, the surveyor was required to record in his field notes the existence of Indian houses or other improvements.  Failure of surveyors to abide by this requirement was common.  If the field notes showed no Indian improvements, the Lands Department in Victoria regarded the land as available for sale, pre-emption, or other forms of alienation.  When failures to record the existence of Indian houses and other improvements were brought to the attention of the Commissioner of Lands, he was unwilling to disturb the equities of non-Indian purchasers.  He noted that some of the lands alienated through use of South African war scrip had been sold two or three times.  Examination of the record shows that a number of these re-sales were between well-known dealers in scrip.  The record also shows that some of the individuals who traded or invested in scrip were individuals who held positions of trust with respect to Indians, that is, government employees and church mission officials.

You will hear that the effect of the issuance of the South African war scrip was that family after family of Wet'suwet'en were forced from their homes.  Wet'suwet'en farms were simply seized; clusters of houses and buildings were razed to the ground.  Wet'suwet'en hunters and trappers and fishermen returned to their homes at the end of summer or in early winter, having completed their season's fishing at Moricetown or Hagwilget, to find white settlers in possession, and able to summon the police to enforce their new, supposed right to these Indian lands.  The bitterness of this appalling invasion of their homes was followed, in many cases, by severe hardship.  With winter coming on families found themselves without shelter.

The names of the Chiefs who were dispossessed appear in government documents of the day under their English names -

*...the surveyor was required to record...the existence of Indian houses or other improvements. Failure...to abide by this requirement was common.*

Photo courtesy of Royal British Columbia Museum

the Christian names that they were given by whites who could
not manage to learn, or chose to disregard, Wet'suwet'en names.
The real names that newcomers ignored included hereditary
Chief names. You will hear much evidence of the dispossession
of Round Lake Tommy, Wah Tah Kwets; Belnai, Medeek;
Mathew Sam, Woos; Auguste Pete, Kwees; and Johnny David,
who is Maxlaxlex and who, in his commissioned evidence,
described what happened:

> In the area of the North Bulkley my father had a big
> smokehouse and when he died the white people burnt it
> down and they kicked me off the land. My dad died in 1908
> and must have been around 30 or 40, and I got a letter from
> Mr. Loring, who was the Indian Agent at Hagwilget. I
> received a letter from him telling me to get off the land and
> he was going to give me acreage in Hagwilget which he
> never did.

To realize that these Christian names represent important
Chiefs in each of the Wet'suwet'en clans leads to another
dimension of the damage done to Wet'suwet'en life by these
early settlers along the Bulkley Valley. Dispossession was not
simply of individuals; those Chiefs were heads of, and
responsible for, large extended families. Family homes and
lands were taken and destroyed. The suffering was therefore on
a larger scale than a list of individual names suggests.

The nature of the dispossession, and the intimidation
with which it was accomplished, will become evident to the
Court from contemporary statements made by the Wet'suwet'en.
Thus, the Court will hear the words of James Yami, Chief
Caspit, as he addressed officials of the Department of Indian
Affairs in 1909:

> The Bulkley River is our river and we get our living
> therefrom. On the lakes are located some of our houses.
> They are small and crude of pattern but we cannot do
> without them. In those houses we have many articles such
> of hunting, trapping, and fishing implements. A white man

*Chief Medeek (left)*          *Chief Wah Tah Kwets (with staff)*

Photo credit: National Museums of Canada

comes along and sets fire to the houses, and on remonstration we are told by the settler: - "You get away from here, I bought this land and if I catch you here again I will have you jailed.

The Wet'suwet'en sought to protest their dispossession in a variety of ways, ranging from confrontation to diplomatic petitions. Violence against whites was averted not only by promises of Indian agents that the land claims of the Wet'suwet'en would be dealt with by government, but by the Wet'suwet'en abiding belief in peaceful resolution of disputes and respect for law. As Chief Caspit stated in 1909:

We always tried to be law abiding. If we want to cut a little firewood we are stopped at once by threats. If we were educated people we would make more complaints. We always give way to the lawless white rather than offend him.

The words of this Wet'suwet'en Chief must not be read as acquiescence to lawlessness. They speak to the importance in the Wet'suwet'en system for respect for other societies - even at the point where they have shown lack of respect- and they speak to a belief in and commitment to the rule of law.

The Wet'suwet'en still hunt and trap on such of their territories as they can safely use, but in travelling the Bulkley Valley, they must pass by farmhouses and fields where white people are now living on land that, in several instances, Wet'suwet'en men and women have themselves cleared and fenced: "unoccupied" farmland that was made available through Boer War scrip. The feelings that surround this large scale appropriation of Wet'suwet'en territory have not faded into the distant past. Nor have these territories disappeared from the Wet'suwet'en system. The Court will hear how ownership of all these places is still identified in the Wet'suwet'en Feast system and the territories are passed on - as always, from generation to generation.

Despite their own dispossession, the Wet'suwet'en and Gitksan Chiefs do not consider as a measure of justice the dispossession of those whites who have settled amongst them. This is evidenced by paragraph 79 of the *Statement of Claim.* The Chiefs have maturely considered this matter and have decided that the title of the settlers and the security of their homes and homesteads shall be confirmed and guaranteed. But this is not to say that the legacies of past dispossession are resolved. As the evidence will reveal, there are outstanding issues pertaining to the relationship between settlers and Indians which include, but are not limited to, access across lands to fishing sites. These must be the subject of negotiated settlement.

# THE NATURE OF THE LEGAL ARGUMENT

The Pleadings in this case assert that the Gitksan and Wet'suwet'en Chiefs have ownership and jurisdiction over their territory; these rights are ones which can only be altered with the consent of the Gitksan and Wet'suwet'en; that in the absence of any settlement of the relationship between them and the colonial, provincial, and federal governments who have come into their territory, and in the absence of any conquest of their peoples and their territory in a just war, their rights as aboriginal peoples have never been extinguished and continue to exist; that those rights are ones recognized by the common law and are proclaimed in the *Royal Proclamation* of 1763; and that those rights are now entrenched in section 35 of the Canadian constitution.

We will be tracing in the evidence the evolution of the legal relationships between the Indian nations and the European governments who have established settlements in North America over the past 400 years. In presenting this evidence, we will be focussing on what we consider to be a central legal issue in this case, the identification of the fundamental principles upon which we assert aboriginal rights are based. This evidence is not to be viewed as an exercise in antiquarianism, nor as interesting historical background - a prologue to the real issues. In the same way as we will be presenting evidence of the history of the Gitksan and Wet'suwet'en people, to enable the Court to understand the development of the fundamental principles by which their societies are ordered, and to determine the scope and content of their aboriginal rights, so the evidence of the legal history will be tendered to identify the fundamental principles which require that Gitksan and Wet'suwet'en rights to ownership and jurisdiction be recognized by a Canadian court.

The importance of the historical matrix to a resolution of the legal issues was made clear by Mr. Justice Dickson (as he then was) in *Kruger and Manuel v. The Queen* (1977), 75 D.L.R.

(3d) 437, when he stated: "claims to aboriginal title are woven with history, legend, politics and moral obligations". The significance of historical evidence has been indelibly underlined by the Supreme Court of Canada in more recent pronouncements dealing with the interpretation of rights entrenched in the Canadian constitution. We will be urging you to adopt a purposive approach to the interpretation to section 35. In *R. v. BIG M DRUG MART* (1985), 1 S.C.R. 295, Chief Justice Dickson articulated the analysis to be undertaken in such a purposive approach to *Charter* rights. Such an analysis requires the Court to analyze "the purpose of the right to freedom question by reference to...the historical origins of the concepts enshrined".

The historical evidence will show that from the earliest stages of colonial settlement, treaties and agreements were entered into with Indian nations for the acquisition of territory and jurisdiction. The process was initiated by the Dutch. These early Dutch treaties date back to the early 17th century and make specific reference to the protocol of acquiring the consent of the Indians in full council, acknowledge the jurisdictional authority of Indian chiefs and recognize as pre-existing the Indian system of land ownership. The establishment of English settlement was also accompanied by agreements with the Indian nations for the acquisition of rights to land. The language in contemporary documents, which will be submitted to this Court, indicates that the colonists did not see their rights pursuant to Royal Charters as giving them title to the land, but only the right to acquire title from the Indians. Thus, you will hear of agreements describing the Indians as "the native inhabitants and true owners" of their territory and of English Royal Commissioners who, in reviewing colonial laws dealing with Indian lands, affirm that "no doubt the country is theirs until they give it or sell it". A review of early colonial documents will also throw important light on the nature of the political relationship between the Indian nations and the British colonists, particularly in terms of the recognition of Indian jurisdictional rights. The evidence will show the extent to which here also changes in jurisdictional arrangements were the subject of negotiated settlement through treaty making.

The evidence will reveal the extent to which, in the 17th and 18th centuries, the formal protocol of treaty-making constituted the legal paradigm for the consolidation and expansion of colonial interests, and the ways in which the fundamental principles underpinning the relationship between the Indians and the British emerged, and were forged, as a result of such treaty making. Of greatest significance, was the principle that Indian rights to their territory be respected, and that their lands could only be alienated to colonial authorities with Indian consent, given by authorized representatives. This principle, as you will see, was to become the centre-piece of the *Royal Proclamation* of 1763 and a founding principle of the common law, as it was articulated by Chief Justice Marshall in the early 19th century.

The evidence will show how the maintenance of the Indian alliance became of critical importance to the British at the outbreak of hostilities with France in the mid-eighteenth century. The Indian nations made it clear that the pre-condition for maintaining that alliance with the British colonies was recognition of their territorial rights, and the redress of frauds and abuses of colonial land speculators. It was largely the inability of the colonial authorities to properly address these vital concerns of the Indians relating to their land rights that led, in 1753, to the Imperial authorities in London taking charge of Indian policy and placing Imperial imprimatur on the affirmation and enforcement of Indian rights to their territories. The evidence will leave you in no doubt that the British authorities came to understand that the integrity of the British Empire in North America, in its continuing struggle with the French for hegemony, was grounded in Indian insistence and British acknowledgement that Indian rights must be respected.

Generations of Canadian students have come to know that 1763 was the year in which the *Treaty of Paris* was signed and the imperial struggle between France and England was resolved in favour of the English. Canadians know that the outcome of the encounter between the English and the French continues to reverberate in contemporary Canadian life regarding the constitutional and political status and role of Quebec in Canadian confederation. But 1763 is also of great importance to

the relationship between Canadians and Indian nations. As with
Quebec, the events of that year continue to resonate with
contemporary legal and constitutional  significance.

On October 7, 1763, what will be referred to throughout
this case as the *Royal Proclamation* of 1763 was issued. You
will be hearing much evidence from the Plaintiffs and the
Defendants regarding the nature, geographical scope, and proper
interpretation of this document. As we understand the
Province's position, they will be arguing that the Proclamation
was conceived at a particular historical juncture at a time of
great Indian unrest; that its measures were designed to ensure
peace on the North American frontier, and to protect the interests
of the British manufacturers, by containing westward expansion
of the existing and newly created colonies. Placing the
Proclamation in a narrow historical framework, they argue that it
was never intended to apply to British Columbia and its
provisions are therefore of no legal or constitutional significance
to the resolution of the issues before this Court.

Our position is different. Based upon the historical
evidence we will be presenting, we say that the Proclamation is
the Imperial affirmation and recognition of the fundamental
principles upon which the legal relationship between Indians and
the Crown are to be resolved. Mr. Justice Hall, in the *Calder*
case referred to the Proclamation as the *Magna Carta* of Indian
rights. Like the *Magna Carta,* the *Royal Proclamation* is not the
source of aboriginal rights but an affirmation of their existence.
Our historical evidence will show how essential features of the
Proclamation are pre-figured in prior treaty making, and thus the
document affirms principles agreed upon by the Indian nations
and the colonial and Imperial authorities.

The principles so affirmed by the *Royal Proclamation*
are first, that Indian nations are recognized by the Crown as
possessing rights to their territory, territory which they are
entitled to possess and which is reserved to them until they
surrender those rights to the Crown. The preamble to the Indian
provisions of the Proclamation reads:

Whereas it is just and reasonable and essential to our interest
and the security of our colonies, that the several Nations or

Tribes of Indians with whom we are connected and who live under our protection, should not be molested or disturbed in the possession of such part of our dominions and territories, as not having been ceded to or purchased by us, are reserved to them as their hunting grounds.

The second principle is that Indian rights are to be acquired by the Crown by consent in accordance with formal treaty making protocol. The Proclamation states:

If at any time any of the said Indians should be inclined to dispose of the said lands, the same shall be purchased only for us, in our name at some public meeting or assembly of the said Indians to be held for the purpose by the Governor or Commander-in-Chief of our colony respectively.

Other provisions of the Proclamation make clear its effect: the Indians are not to be disturbed in possession of their lands; representatives of the Crown are not to make grants of unsurrendered lands; private individuals cannot purchase lands from the Indians; private individuals settled on lands which have not been acquired in accordance with proscribed procedures are to leave; and if the Crown wishes to make use of Indian lands for the purpose of settlement, those lands must be purchased by the Crown at a meeting between the representatives of the Crown and the Indian nations.

In contrast to the Province's position, we will argue that the recognition in the *Royal Proclamation* of aboriginal rights and of a process by which those rights can be transferred to the Crown, conditioned upon the consent of the Indians, are not transient notions, limited in time and geography by a narrow reading of the events of 1763. We will be arguing that, as a basic constitutional document, the Proclamation must be given a large and liberal interpretation; that placed in its proper historical context, it confirmed pre-existing law and policy and serves as a codification of that law and policy to be applied as British settlement advanced westward.

We will be presenting evidence as to the contemporary interpretation of the Proclamation by those colonial officials charged with its implementation. We will also be presenting extensive evidence of the over 500 treaties which have been made between the Crown and the Indian nations within Canada since 1763, treaties which we say are the best evidence of the Proclamation's prospective application.

We will be arguing that the *Royal Proclamation* placed legal and constitutional limitations on the authority of colonial governors to grant Indian lands, except where those lands were surrendered with Indian consent, in accordance with the Proclamation's prescribed procedures. We will further argue that a proper interpretation of the *Colonial Laws Validity Act* requires that all colonial enactments must be read down to be consistent with the operation of the *Royal Proclamation.* We will argue therefore that the colonial proclamations and ordinances relied on by the Province of British Columbia, in their *Statement of Defence,* to extinguish the aboriginal rights of the Gitksan and Wet'suwet'en, cannot have that legal effect.

However, our case does not hang on a single legal hinge that the *Royal Proclamation* applies to British Columbia. Paralleling our argument on the *Royal Proclamation,* we say that the fundamental principles which are reflected in the Proclamation have also become embodied in the common law. The legal relationship of the Indian nations with Britain and the United States was the subject of extensive judicial consideration, in a series of judgements of the United States Supreme Court, written by Chief Justice Marshall in the early 19th century. You will be referred extensively to these, as they have come to be regarded by the highest courts of Britain, Canada, and other Commonwealth countries as the authoritative decisions on the common law of aboriginal rights. In reaching his decisions, Chief Justice Marshall engaged in an extensive analysis of British Crown and Indian relationships in North America. As such, they have direct legal relevance to Canada. This point has been clearly articulated by Canadian judges, most recently by the Supreme Court of Canada in *Guerin.*

The judgement of Chief Justice Marshall in *Worcester v. Georgia* is properly regarded as the centre-piece of the common law of aboriginal rights. In *Worcester,* Chief Justice Marshall espoused as fundamental to the common law a "universal conviction that the Indian nations possessed a full right to the lands they occupied until right should be extinguished by the United States with their consent".

It is more than an interesting historical coincidence that this statement of common law principles regarding aboriginal rights was made within a decade of Peter Ogden's first journey to the ancient Wet'suwet'en village of Kya Wiget and his recognition of the Wet'suwet'en Chiefs as "men of property".

As you will hear, *Worcester v. Georgia* came before the Supreme Court in the wake of attempts by the State of Georgia to take over the lands and jurisdiction of the Cherokee nation in violation of a treaty between the Cherokee nation and the United States. The litigation was referred to in 1847 by a New Zealand judge, Mr. Justice Chapman, in a search to identify what he called "certain established principles of law applicable to...the intercourse of civilized nations, and especially of Great Britain, with the aboriginal natives of America and other countries during the last two centuries". Mr. Justice Chapman's search for fundamental principles yielded this conclusion:

> The practice of extinguishing native titles by fair purchases is certainly more than two centuries old. It has long been adopted by the government in our American colonies, and by that of the United States. It is now part of the law of the land...In the case of *The Cherokee Nation v. State of Georgia* the Supreme Court through its protective decision over the Plaintiff-nation against a gross attempt at spoilation; calling to its aid, throughout every portion of its judgment, the principles of the common law as applied and adopted from the earliest times by the colonial laws...whatever may be the opinion of jurists as to the strength or weakness of their native title...it cannot be too solemnly asserted that it is entitled to be respected, that it cannot be extinguished (at least in time of peace) otherwise than by free consent of the native occupiers.

We will be arguing that, as with the *Royal Proclamation,* the common law of England as it was received in British Columbia, imposed a legal obligation on the Crown to acquire lands for settlement with the consent of the Indian nations.

We will be placing before this Court evidence which documents the intention of the British Crown that the rights of the Indians of British Columbia be respected in accordance with the obligations imposed by the *Royal Proclamation* and the common law. You will hear of the instructions issued to Captain James Cook in 1776. On Cook's third voyage he explored what is now the coast of British Columbia and British claims to the land rest in part on Cook's discoveries. Cook was thus instructed:

> You are also with the consent of the natives to take possession in the name of the King of Great Britain of convenient situations in such countries as you may discover, that have not already been discovered or visited by any other European power.

You will read the instructions given to Captains Nathaniel Portlock and George Dixon to purchase land from the Indians on which to build trading posts which they were sent to establish at Nootka Sound on the west coast of Vancouver Island.

You will hear evidence that with the establishment of the colony of Vancouver Island as a British settlement in 1849, the Crown grant of land to the Hudson's Bay Company carried with it the same burden of extinguishing Indian title as that which rested on the Crown. The evidence of the early history of the colony of Vancouver Island will show how James Douglas, as Governor of Vancouver Island, concluded a series of treaties for the acquisition of Indian territories required for settlement purposes. The analysis of evidence drawn from contemporary documents will show that these treaties were understood to be in conformity with the law and policy of recognizing Indian title, and of extinguishing such title only with the consent of the Indians. That same evidence will show that both the Imperial and the colonial authorities contemplated that treaty making would be continued. You will be referred to a petition from the House of Assembly in Victoria forwarded to the Duke of

Newcastle in which funds are requested to extinguish Indian title
to certain lands in the colony of Vancouver Island.  In his letter
of transmittal, Governor Douglas noted that the Indians expected
that settlement would proceed only with their consent and that
the failure to make proper arrangements boded ill for the  future
of the colony.  Douglas' words have a contemporary significance
for this case:

> As the native Indian population of Vancouver Island have
> distinct ideas of property and land, and mutually recognize
> their several exclusive possessory rights in certain districts,
> they would not fail to regard the occupation of such portions
> of the colony by White settlers, unless with the full consent
> of the proprietary tribes, as national wrongs.

Evidence will be presented to this Court showing that
while then, as now, public opinion was divided on this issue,
there existed a considerable body of public opinion that
recognized the existence of native title to their territories, and
regarded it as a matter of justice and the upholding of the honour
of the Crown, to negotiate for the surrender of Indian lands
required for settlement.

It is in the historical context of this evidence that you
will be able to assess the strength of the Province's argument that
ordinances and proclamations passed by Douglas and the House
of Assembly during this period were intended to extinguish
Indian title unilaterally, without fair purchase, without Indian
consent.

You will hear extensive evidence regarding the policies
of the colonial administrations who succeeded to the governance
of British Columbia after James Douglas' retirement.  From
1864 until the admission of British Columbia into confederation
in 1871, Indian policy came under the influence of Joseph
Trutch.  You will find in his views on Indians and Indian rights
the historical source of the *Statement of Defence* of the
Province of British Columbia.  His ghost rattles within their
pleadings.

Not to put too fine a point on it, Joseph Trutch was an
archetypical colonialist who represented the ideology of the

frontier with all its implicit and explicit assumptions regarding the superiority of European civilization and the inferiority of native people. You will hear how he arrived in British Columbia in 1859 with eight years experience behind him in the United States as a surveyor and farmer. After working for five years in British Columbia as a surveyor and engineer, he became the colony's Chief Commissioner of Lands and Works. His interest in the gold colony in the early days was in building roads and bridges, in surveying townships, and establishing farms, and in amassing a personal fortune.

For Joseph Trutch, Indians and Indian rights stood in the way of his view of civilization. His attitude towards Indian rights was expressed in the statement he made in 1867 that:

> the Indians have really no right to the lands they claim, nor are they of any actual value or utility to them, and I cannot see why they should...retain these lands to the prejudice of the general interest of the colony or be allowed to make a market of them either to government or to individuals.

Two years prior to this, in responding to Indian land claims in the Thompson River area, Joseph Trutch responded that he was quite:

> satisfied from my own observations that the claims of the Indians over tracts of land, and on which they assume to exercise ownership, but of which they make no real use, operate very materially to prevent settlement and cultivation.

To Joseph Trutch, Indian life was invisible and their rights were to be disregarded as obstacles to progress.

Our evidence will direct your attention to the terrible paradox of history by which this archetypical colonialist became recognized as an expert on the Indian question and was called upon to defend the Province's position on Indian policy, in the face of criticism that it disregarded Indian rights, contrary to law. You will hear how in 1870, Joseph Trutch took the opportunity to claim that British Columbia had always denied the idea of aboriginal title. He wrote that:

> the title of the Indians in fee of the public lands, or any portion thereof, has never been acknowledged by government, but, on the contrary, is distinctly denied.

Not surprisingly, Trutch does not explain why the Vancouver Island House of Assembly should ask the Imperial government in 1861 for money to extinguish an Indian title, the existence of which they did not recognize.

Joseph Trutch's self-serving memorandum of 1870 provides the script for British Columbia's position in this Court today. It is a script which has been read to the Indians of British Columbia over the past 100 years. Its repetition does not make it right either as a matter of fact or as a matter of law.

In our argument we will be submitting to you that the period of 1864-1871 is properly to be viewed as an attempt by colonial administrators to flout the fundamental principle embodied in the *Royal Proclamation* and the common law, and it should be exposed for what it represents - the distortion of fundamental principles of justice in the interests of racism.

In the course of our evidence and argument, you will be referred to the protectorate or trust responsibility of the Crown. In the *Royal Proclamation* of 1763 the preamble refers to the nations of Indians "with whom we are connected and who live under our protection". We will be submitting that this protectorate was not by way of diminution of the rights of the Indian nations to exercise their jurisdiction over their territory (except in accordance with treaty making), but was conceived as a legal and political measure to ensure the protection of Indian rights from such diminution. As our evidence of the history of the period preceding the *Royal Proclamation* will demonstrate, the need for protection of Indian rights from abuse and fraud by whites at the frontier of the colonies, and the inability or unwillingness of the local governments to protect such rights, spurred the consolidation and codification of Imperial recognition of Indian rights.

Nor did this cease to be an important concern of the Imperial authorities after 1763.  In the evidence you will be referred to the report of the *Select Committee* of the British House of Commons in 1837 which predicted a potential conflict of interest situation should the jurisdiction to administer Crown obligations regarding Indians fall to the legislatures of the colonies.  In considering the measures to be adopted to guard against this, the report stated that Britain held a trust:

> peculiarly belonging and appropriate to the executive government as administered either in this country or by the governors of their respective colonies.  This is not a trust which could conveniently be confided to the local legislatures.

The evidence regarding the policies of Joseph Trutch will demonstrate that the *Select Committee's* concerns were well-founded.  It was for the reason given by the *Select Committee* that jurisdiction of Indians and lands reserved for Indians was vested in the federal government in section 91(24) *Constitution Act, 1867*.  We will be presenting legal argument that section 91(24) in conjunction with section 109 of the *Constitution Act, 1867* provides a framework for the constitutional protection of aboriginal rights.

But constitutions are not self-executing.  The federal government, in the exercise of its constitutional obligations, and in particular its protectorate role, did shortly after British Columbia's admission into confederation exercise its power of disallowance of provincial laws on the basis that the *B.C. Land Act of 1874* did not adequately recognize the aboriginal rights of the native people of British Columbia.  You will be referred to the opinion of the then Minister of Justice in which he says:

> There is no shadow of a doubt, that from the earliest times England has always felt it imperative to meet the Indians in Council, and to obtain surrenders of tracts of Canada as from time to time such were required for the purposes of settlement.

The Minister of Justice went on to recite the provisions of the *Royal Proclamation* and concluded that:

> The undersigned feels that he cannot do otherwise than advise that Act in question is objectionable, as tending to deal with lands which are assumed to be the absolute property of the Province, an assumption which completely ignores, as applicable to the Indians of British Columbia, the honour and good faith which the Crown has, in all other cases since its sovereignty in North America, dealt with their various Indian tribes.

Unfortunately, as our evidence will show, the later history of the federal government's exercise of its protectorate or trust responsibility was informed more by a concern for the protection of federal-provincial relationships than the protection of the interests of the Indians from provincial incursions. The *Statement of Defence* filed by the Attorney General of Canada constitutes the best evidence of the federal government's contemporary understanding of its protectorate responsibility.

The extent to which Indian rights have been subordinated to federal-provincial interests is well illustrated by the debate leading up to the passage of section 35 of the *Constitution Act, 1982*. The decision to entrench aboriginal and treaty rights in the constitution was first reached on January 30, 1981. In November of that year, the federal government agreed to delete the aboriginal and treaty rights clause in exchange for broader political accord with the provinces. That about-face created a storm of protest, extensive lobbying and lengthy negotiations which ultimately led to a new agreement to entrench the present form of section 35.

The speeches in Parliament, by leaders of all three political parties at the time of that agreement, show that the legislative objective of including aboriginal and treaty rights in the *Constitution of Canada* was to restore the honour of the Crown in its dealings with the Indian nations.

The Rt. Hon. Joe Clark, Leader of the Opposition:

I want to speak for a moment, if I might, of the nature of that duty, the nature of our responsibility to the aboriginal people of the country. One in this nationalist age would be reluctant to quote a poet from the United States, except perhaps in the case of aboriginal title, because the aboriginals were here before the United States or Canada was, before the forty-ninth parallel meant anything more than another widening in the trees. I am struck by the words of Robert Frost who came late to this continent. He said:

"The land was ours before we were the lands."

Mr. Frost was speaking of the white population, not the natives. The land of this continent belonged to, was used by, the original people well before the concept of land took root as something that was possessed and parceled out. Land, to the natives, was where you lived, where you worked and where you took your nature. It was heritage, not just territory. In a very real sense, land and people were the same.

We took that away, we who came later. We took it away as an inevitable consequence of our civilization and the compensation we offered was often meagre, often mean, sometimes nothing at all. But the original people were here before our civilization. Our treatment, our meagre, mean treatment of them, has increased our obligation, not diminished it.

We cannot reverse history, but we can take account of it. A minimum step must be for this Parliament to put in a document that deals with the rights of our people and to acknowledge at least the particular rights of our first people to draw their life and their culture from what we made our land.

Hon. John C. Munroe - then Minister of Indian Affairs:

Members of the House, I cannot overemphasize the significance that I place on the events of the last couple of days in view of the outcome. The distance that native people have come in those few short days, by gaining recognition for their aboriginal and treaty rights in what is soon to become the highest expression of the law of this land, is immeasurable at this time. However, I predict that history will prove it to be a giant step...

I want the Indian people especially to understand why I feel as I do. To be sure, the contrast between my disappointment of a few days ago and my mood today is uplifting. But that is not the only reason. Hon. members, we are here today in the House of Commons with a motion that proposed to accord to native peoples a unique status in the highest law of the land....

Notwithstanding the inclusion of s. 35, Indian nations from Alberta and the Maritimes took a case to England to urge Britain to refuse patriation, on the basis that Britain had not formally transferred Crown obligations to Canada with the Indian consent. In refusing the application, the Court of Appeal held that Crown obligations had passed to Canada at least with the passage of the *Statute of Westminster.* Lord Denning said this about his view of the effect of s. 35:

It seems to me that the *Canada Bill* itself does all that can be done to protect the rights and freedoms of the aboriginal peoples of Canada. It entrenches them as part of the Constitution, so that they cannot be diminished or reduced except by the prescribed procedure and by the prescribed majorities. In addition, it provides for a conference at the highest level to be held so as to settle exactly what their rights are. That is most important, for they are very ill-defined at the moment.

There is nothing, so far as I can see, to warrant any distrust by the Indians of the Government of Canada. But, in case there should be, the discussion in this case will strengthen their hand so as to enable them to withstand any onslaught. They will be able to say that their rights and freedoms have been guaranteed to them by the Crown - originally by the Crown in respect of the United

Kingdom - now by the Crown in respect of Canada - but, in any case, by the Crown. No Parliament should do anything to lessen the worth of these guarantees. They should be honoured by the Crown in respect of Canada "so long as the sun rises and the river flows". That promise must never be broken

As this Court is aware, through constitutional amendment to section 37, a series of federal-provincial conferences have been held with participation of the aboriginal peoples of Canada. What emerged from these conferences as the overarching concern of the aboriginal peoples was to ensure the entrenchment of their right to self-government. In March of this year, the conferences ended with no accord. The exhaustion of this process has made it clear to the Gitksan and Wet'suwet'en that there is not the political will in this country to come to grips with the historical and legal reality of aboriginal rights. The politicians have, in effect, deferred the matter to the courts.

As our evidence will show, the subject of aboriginal rights in British Columbia has its own history of being deferred. Indeed, the decision by the Supreme Court of Canada in the *Calder* case, in which the court split evenly on the substantive issue of whether the aboriginal title of the Nishga Indians had been lawfully extinguished, was widely regarded as a judicial deferral of the issue back to the politicians. The Government of British Columbia, however, has taken a narrow technical view of that decision as confirming its intransigent position that the Indians of British Columbia do not have existing aboriginal rights. The B.C. Court of Appeal in the *Meares Island* case has made it clear, not only that the Province's position on the effect of *Calder* is misconceived, but also that the issue is to be deferred no longer. Mr. Justice Seaton stated:

There is a problem about tenure that has not been attended to in the past. We are being asked to ignore the problem as others have ignored it. I am not willing to do that.

In bringing this case to court, the Gitksan and Wet'suwet'en chiefs are not, however, simply relitigating the issues raised in *Calder*, nor are they re-presenting the same evidence and argument. In *Calder* there was no argument about the scope of aboriginal rights. The issue was limited to the Nishga rights of ownership to their territory; there was no claim to jurisdiction or authority over it. In *Calder* the legal argument relating to extinguishment turned on a debate between whether aboriginal rights could be extinguished implicitly by the provisions of the colonial ordinances and proclamations cited in the Province's *Statement of Defence* or whether such rights could only be extinguished by specific legislation expressly directed to that purpose. There was no argument that aboriginal rights could only be extinguished with Indian consent.

It is, however, the nature of the evidence which will be presented to this Court that distinguishes it most from the *Calder* case. It is a remarkable feature of aboriginal rights litigation that some of the most important cases have been argued in the absence of Indian evidence. Indeed, one of the leading Canadian authorities, the *St. Catherine's Milling* case, was decided in the context of a federal-provincial dispute over lands which had been surrendered in a treaty in accordance with the procedures of the *Royal Proclamation*, so that there was no representation of the Indian interest at all, let alone any Indian evidence before the court. Other cases have proceeded on agreed statement of facts. The *Calder* case proceeded on a combination of agreement of fact and limited Indian evidence. No court in grappling with the issues of aboriginal rights has had the opportunity which this Court will have of hearing Indian witnesses describe their history, the nature of their society, their institutions, and their legal order from which their rights to ownership and jurisdiction are derived.

The evidence of the Chiefs will not only provide you with an understanding of the substance of their rights, but it will also inform your judgement on the Province's principal defence in this case. That defence is that the assertion of ownership 100 years ago in colonial ordinances and proclamations by implication has the legal effect of extinguishing the ownership and jurisdiction of a civilization that has existed for more than 5000 years. In a case involving the search for fundamental principles for determining the legal relationship between the

Gitksan and Wet'suwet'en and the provincial and federal
governments, we will be arguing that there is no room for a legal
doctrine that countenances the extinguishment of the rights upon
which a civilization is based through the stroke of a colonial pen.
In one of your own judgements, you referred to the common law
as "a statement of the accumulated wisdom of history - a
dynamic force which is always ready to respond to the
reasonable requirements of civilization". We will be submitting
to you that the principle of Indian consent to the acquisition by
other governments of ownership and authority over their
territory represents a fundamental principle of the common law.
It was fundamental to the integrity of the British Empire in 1763.
It is no less fundamental to the integrity of Canada in 1987.

    We have already referred to the judgement of Mr. Justice
Dickson in *Kruger and Manuel v. The Queen* and his Lordship's
reference to aboriginal rights being interwoven with history,
legend, moral obligations, and politics. By granting the
declarations the Plaintiffs seek in this case, the Court will be
acknowledging the real history of the Gitksan and Wet'suwet'en
and ensure their rightful place in the history books of British
Columbia and Canada; by granting the declarations the Court
will also put legal fibre into the moral obligations of the
provincial and federal governments. But most important of all,
by declaring that the Plaintiffs have rights of ownership and
jurisdiction over their territories, and that these rights have not
been extinguished, this Court will be charging the provincial and
federal governments with the legal and constitutional obligation
to negotiate with the Gitksan and Wet'suwet'en a just settlement
of their relationship on the basis that they have existing
aboriginal rights.

    You are used to charging juries. The charge we are
asking you to make in this case is perhaps the most important
one any judge in British Columbia has ever been asked to make.
From this perspective, it is appropriate that you sit as the Chief
Justice of the Supreme Court. But challenges of a similar order
of magnitude have been made to other Chief Justices to affirm
the legal rights of native people in the face of government
disregard. We have already referred you to the judgements of
Chief Justice Marshall. In the face of an attempted

dispossession of the Cherokee nation, he affirmed that the Cherokees were indeed a nation of Indians with rights to their territory. That affirmation was not enough in the face of the doctrine of "Manifest Destiny" to stop the dispossession of the Cherokees under the guise of a fraudulent treaty and their forced march along the "Trail of Tears" to Oklahoma. The Gitksan and the Wet'suwet'en have also suffered the effects of dispossession from significant parts of their homelands. But the dispossession and the destruction of their territories must stop from this point on, and legal acknowledgement must be made of the extent of the Province of British Columbia's disregard of the fundamental principles of justice upon which aboriginal rights are based, and from which a just settlement of the relationship between the Gitksan and Wet'suwet'en and the provincial and federal governments must evolve.

In the *Meares Island* case, Mr. Justice McFarlane acutely observed that litigation is "but a part of the whole of a process which will ultimately find its solution in a reasonable exchange between governments and the Indian nations". But litigation is a necessary and vital part. This case offers you an historic opportunity, based on evidence no other court has ever heard, to render judgement that will move Canada closer to the achievement of a true Confederation which includes its founding Indian nations.

# THE CLOSING STATEMENT OF THE GITKSAN AND WET'SUWET'EN HEREDITARY CHIEFS IN THE SUPREME COURT OF BRITISH COLUMBIA

By
Gisday Wa A.K.A. Alfred Joseph
Delgam Uukw A.K.A. Earl Muldoe
Yagalahl A.K.A. Dora Wilson-Kenni
Maas Gaak A.K.A. Don Ryan
May 14, 1990

We, the Gitksan and Wet'suwet'en people, are in the court to state the truth of the ownership and jurisdiction we exercise over our territories.

Three years have passed since we made our opening statements to this court. At that time, you did not know who Delgam Uukw and Gisday Wa were. Now, this court knows I am Gisday Wa, a Wet'suwet'en Chief who has responsibility for the House of Kaiyexwaniits of the Gitdumden. I have explained how my House holds the Biiwenii Ben Territory and had the privilege of showing it to you. Long ago my ancestors encountered the spirit of that land and accepted the responsibility to care for it. In return, the land has fed the House members and those whom the Chiefs permitted to harvest its resources. Those who have obeyed the laws of respect and balance have prospered there.

I am Delgam Uukw, the third since this trial started. I also have obligations to my House and the territories of my House. You have heard oral histories of the Gitksan and Wet'suwet'en that tell of the many groups that migrated into our territories. Many stayed, contributing to our culture, acknowledging the authority of our Chiefs and obeying our laws.

Of all these groups, only the Europeans failed to recognize our ownership and jurisdiction. This court now has an opportunity to redress this situation.

We, the hereditary Chiefs, decided against wearing blankets and regalia in this courtroom because we believe that our authority would not be respected by the government lawyers. Under our law, disrespect for people and for their territory requires compensation.

We, the Gitksan and Wet'suwet'en, must be compensated for loss of the land's present integrity and for the loss of economic rents.

We ask that the court not only acknowledge our ownership and jurisdiction over the land, but also restore it to a form adequate for nature to heal in terms of restoration. We would like to see clearcuts and plantations returned to forests, contaminated rivers and lakes returned to their original pristine state, reservoirs of drowned forests returned to living lakes, and life-sustaining flows to diverted rivers.

We realize that the true financial value of this compensation for restoration would bankrupt both the federal and provincial governments. Compensation must remain an ongoing obligation of the federal and provincial governments "until our hearts are satisfied".

However, this compensation should not be viewed by this court as an alternative to the acknowledgment of our ownership and jurisdiction of our land. We do not want financial compensation without the recognition of our authority over our territories.

We are asking you to make declarations on Gitksan and Wet'suwet'en aboriginal title. We, the Gitksan and Wet'suwet'en people, own our lands.

I will identify those areas where the powers of the province and the federal governments need to be restrained in order for us to exercise our responsibilities under aboriginal title.

First, we the Chiefs must have our authority recognized in order to exercise our responsibility to protect the land for the future and to conserve resources. We must have the power to manage all human activity that brings change to the land, air and water on all of our territories.

Second, to enable each House to provide for its members and all those living in their territory, the Chiefs must have control over the local economy by managing natural resource allocations within their territories. This would include licensing, leasing and permitting. As well, royalties and taxation payments from resource use on our territories must be paid to us.

It is not our intention to exert any powers over the non-Gitksan and Wet'suwet'en people living in our territories. Fee-simple lands held by third parties as of October, 1984, would be exempt from this resource allocation.

We see the pulling back of these central government powers as being the minimum required to restore not only individual self-reliance but also community self-reliance. We have presented you with ample evidence of the effects on our land resulting from government resource management. We have also given evidence of the effect that centralized economic management and government welfare has had on our people. The governments' system does not work. We, the hereditary Chiefs, believe we can change the situation under our laws and practices through our authority.

Our system of government is as powerful today, and will be as powerful tomorrow, as it was one hundred or ten thousand years ago. You have heard both ancient and modern histories tell of how our system has remained relevant through the evolving ecological, cultural and economic circumstances in which our people have found themselves. To say we disobey our laws and ignore our Chiefs' authority because we change a piece of technology, or use our land in a different way, is a desperate argument.

This case, then, is about learning from the past so we can repair the present and pass on a healthier land to our grandchildren. It is not about retrieving frozen rights from a nineteenth century ice-box.

Our aboriginal title is found in common law and takes precedence over the provincial crown. We do not have to, and will not, surrender our aboriginal title in order to be recognized by the federal government. We are self-governing.

However, we see a layering of responsibilities among the Gitksan and Wet'suwet'en, the federal government, and the provincial government being resolved in an ongoing series of negotiations. Given the strong imperative for the Gitksan and Wet'suwet'en, British Columbia, and Canada to have social and economic activities continue within our territories, consensus on the necessary political and administrative framework must be found.

We are asking this court to properly apply common law. We want a declaration of recognition and affirmation of our continued ownership and jurisdiction. We will not surrender or diminish our title and rights. We do not request a "right" to use and occupy the land, and we refuse extended reserve lands. We will decide what our future relationship will be with Canada and British Columbia on this basis.

We ask nothing more than what should have occurred prior to confederation, and prior to this providence entering confederation. We are here to right the wrongs that have been occurring for over one hundred years. This court has the power recognize and affirm Gitksan and Wet'suwet'en ownership and jurisdiction.

# A TRAVESTY OF JUSTICE

The decision of the Supreme Court of British Columbia on *Delgam Uukw et. al. v The Queen*, the longest running aboriginal title rights case in the country, was handed down this morning. As it reads, Mr. Justice Allan MacEachern has handed down a political decision that clearly demonstrates that the interests of the courts in British Columbia are not those of justice, but of the legalistic manipulation of facts and history to justify the continued sanctioned marginalization of aboriginal people to the point that their existing rights, as protected by the Canadian constitution, do not apply in British Columbia.

In a turn of retrogressive legal thinking, this judge is attempting to push back justice for native people of Canada at least twenty years. This has been done by either ignoring or rejecting legal gains made in the last few years by native people all over the country. This judge goes as far as saying that native people, especially the Gitksan and Wet'suwet'en, are economically marginalized because they live on reserves and that the only hope of change can come if they leave and assimilate into the mainstream. This is the 1969 White Paper, a policy long rejected by successive federal regimes.

Even at the introduction of the document, this judge states "…I have been brutal." Indeed this is an understatement. The volume of evidence this judge rejects in respect to the continued ownership and jurisdiction of the Gitksan and Wet'suwet'en territories, the details of cultural organisation, of the language, of their whole cultures, is amazing. Was this judge actually there through the whole of the trial? It seems not. After three years of hearing testimony, the judge even rejects the idea that the Gitksan and Wet'suwet'en cultures were and are complex and sophisticated, instead asserting that thousands of years of social development happened since European contact.

As amazing as this seems, it becomes more so. This judge rejects the findings of the Supreme Court of Canada in *Sparrow* in terms of aboriginal rights in general and rights to fishing in particular, opting instead to impose his own very narrow view. For instance, it appears from this judge's statement that aboriginal rights to fish extend onto tidal waters only, and further than that, the actions of this province when still a colony were sufficient, it seems, to extinguish even this right. This judge goes on from this reasoning to extrapolate that the colony was able to extinguish all aboriginal rights, including those to land, by some sort of fiat that required neither the knowledge or the consent of the native people living in what is now British Columbia. The reasoning of the Supreme Court of Canada on this in *Sparrow* seems to have been wholly ignored. This judge concludes, more or less, that prior to contact, native people in British Columbia lead a life that was nasty, brutish and short and that it took European contact to make them culturally self-aware and to give them any sense of territoriality. In short, prior to contact, this judge thinks native people were little more than fairly bright animals.

This judgement is full of similar arguments that either debase and belittle aboriginal people and their cultures and certainly render them subject to European cultural domination in total, or that attempt to refute previously established legal precedents. According to this judge, it seems that even the Constitution does not obtain in B.C. It is indeed a handy thing, when one lives in a federal structure, to be able to cast aside laws and rights that do not fit into the political imperative. The Constitution is the law of the land, except when this judge is presiding.

The tone this judge is attempting to set is that native people in B.C. have no rights, no real culture that could in any way be equated with what was imported from Europe, and certainly no say in what happens to their land. When the Europeans came, it was game over. If native people think they have been denied justice, too bad. Given what could have been a great day for justice in this country, we come away with nothing. MacEachern's judgement is a travesty based on the economic imperatives of a province driven by exploitation of people and resources. He has rectified nothing.

Perhaps he expects the native rights struggle in B.C. and Canada to magically end because of this decision. Instead, in his myopia, he has fuelled the causes of racism. Judgements of this kind foster only enmity. Aboriginal people will protect their rights and will force this agenda. The actuality, or threat of violent force by the state cannot keep people down. It has not worked in South Africa, and it did not work last summer at Oka. Justice will be served in the end and this province may expect considerable unrest, protest, and direct political action if the government attempts to use this small, silly judgement to inform policy. An appeal can be expected.

**Chief Medeek, Wolf Clan, Moricetown**
*From a painting by W. Langdon Kihn*

Photo credit: National Museums of Canada